Haskell Institute: 19th Century Stories of Sacrifice and Survival

With a Haskell Cemetery Walking Tour

Interpreted by Theresa Milk, Ph.D.

Mammoth Publications
Lawrence, Kansas 66044

To the Reader: Thank you for taking the time to read this story of stories. Please share the stories with others—that is one way to honor those whose stories remain untold.

ISBN 0–9761773–8–2
published by
Mammoth Publications
1916 Stratford Rd. Lawrence, Kansas 66044

Direct inquiries and orders to
www.mammothlpublications.com

Cover Photo: Haskell students, circa 1884, All photographs courtesy of Haskell Archives, Haskell Cultural Center and Museum, Haskell Indian Nations University, 155 Indian Ave., Lawrence, Kansas 66046

Lovingly dedicated to the memory of

Elijah, May, Ada, Willie, Josiah

and all the others
who sacrificed for our future

Acknowledgements

First of all, I would like to thank Bobbi Rahder for putting my feet on the path of this particular journey through the past. If she had not hired me during the summer of 2002 as a museum technician, the stories contained within might have remained buried. I would also like to thank Marilyn Finke at the National Archives in Kansas City, Missouri, for all of the assistance she so willingly offered. Likewise, the volunteers at the State Historical Society in Topeka and the Haskell Cultural Center and Museum were also helpful in this endeavor.

At the same time, I could not have completed this task were it not for my family. My husband Orville and my children, Natasha, Kyle, Samantha and Sommer, were patient and supportive, in spite of the fact that I spent many, many hours away from them. Many a night and weekend they had to fend for themselves, while I went to the library or spent time locked away reading and writing; for all that, they have my deepest gratitude, love and respect. And of course, I must acknowledge my grandchildren: Ku tho-he, Jazymne, Dream, Bishop, Logan, Nikki, Stormy, Damon, and Bella, for they are my future.

I would like to thank my instructors at Haskell, for they believed in me and my capabilities; ultimately, they made me believe in myself. Were it not for their faith, help and understanding along the way, I might not have made it to this point. I also need to acknowledge the support staff at Haskell, for they too helped me in many different ways during my journey. Additionally, I do need to thank my advisor, Dr. John Rury at the University of Kansas, for allowing me to pursue my passion.

Mammoth Publications and the author are grateful for the generous contribution of Blue Heron Typesetters, Lawrence, Kansas.

Most importantly, I would like to take time to recognize the students of Haskell, past, present and future. Those from the past have taught me the meaning of pride, honor, respect, sacrifice, and survival. It is my hope that in sharing their stories, the present and future Haskell students will be inspired and push themselves to their highest capability, just as the earliest students did.

TABLE OF CONTENTS

Forward

Over 120 years ago, in September, 1884, an institution with a rather generic name—The United States Indian Industrial Training School—officially opened for business just outside of the growing community of Lawrence, Kansas. Even before it opened, the government-run, off-reservation boarding school was affectionately termed Haskell Institute, a tribute to Congressman Dudley Haskell, who was instrumental in ensuring the school's location in the "Athens of the West," the title given to Lawrence. The name "Haskell Institute" was officially recognized in 1890, and as the institution and its mission evolved over time, from assimilation and industrial training in the late 19th century to education and scholarship in the early 21st century, so has the name evolved until today it is known as Haskell Indian Nations University.[1]

Throughout that span of time, thousands of Native individuals have passed through the doors of the institution. It often has been said by Haskell alumni that they can go anywhere in the United States with visible Haskell memorabilia (i.e. tee-shirt, jacket, hat, etc.), and, inevitably, they will be approached by someone who vocalizes some type of connection to the institution. (I can attest to this fact from personal experience.) Invariably, there will be an exchange of information between the individuals—a greeting and some type of acknowledgement of the institution and the speaker's connection to Haskell. For example, alumni might hear, "I attended Haskell back in 1973 when it was a junior college" or "My grandmother went to Haskell way back when" or even, "My mom and dad met at Haskell." And sometimes one individual shares a little piece of Haskell history with another. This is oral tradition. These stories that are shared sometimes get passed along in a general form. Stories are told and re-told. These stories are a part of the history of Haskell even as they remain unwritten.

As expected, most of the stories that are told nowadays are from the middle to late 20th century. Unfortunately, there are very few stories that are told—oral or otherwise—about students in the earliest years at Haskell, the late 19th century. There are, of course, a number of reasons for the absence of student stories from that time frame, most notably, the lack of documents and verifiable information regarding members of this group—a problem common to any research conducted on the pre-20th century "common man."

In Haskell's case, there are only scattered bits of information, usually in the form of institutional records available on Native students of the late-1800s. Consequently, researching the time frame is challenging—but it can be done. In fact, the research in this text uncovers a surprising number of stories about Haskell students from 1884–1900. Some of the stories are very short and others are detailed, but all together they bring another perspective to the known history of 19th century Haskell Institute. Of course, there have been a number of historical narratives previously done on Haskell. However, the existing narratives include few, if any, 19th century Haskell *student* stories. Furthermore, none of the existing narratives include most of the stories in this current study.

Given the inherent difficulty of 19th century research, historians might assume there is not enough information available to tell stories of 19th century Haskell students, beyond what has already been told. I considered these assumptions before I began this project, but I could not shake the presence of two questions in my own mind—have the stories of early Haskell students really been lost in time? Can any student stories of 19th century Haskell be salvaged from the meager bits of information that were recorded in various written documents that have survived over time? Those two questions would take me on a fascinating journey through many pieces of so many lives, a journey that illuminated such courage, strength and resilience of the 19th century Haskell students. This is a journey that found some beautiful stories of sacrifice and survival of the Native peoples of another time. In a very real way, the stories are resurrecting voices of the unheard. These are stories that needed to be found, stories that needed to be remembered, stories that needed to be told and re-told.

My first connection with Haskell came in the form of stories shared by my husband about his time at Haskell Indian Junior College, where he earned his Associates Degree in Auto Mechanics in 1984. I could see in his eyes, when he was sharing direct memories, that he had a certain fondness for the institution. Almost a decade after I heard the first story, the connection became personal when I arrived at Haskell Indian Nations University as a non-traditional student in the fall of 1998. Over the next three years I earned two degrees, an Associate of Arts in Liberal Arts and a Bachelor of Arts in American Indian Studies; and I learned the basic rigor, expectations and core knowledge of academic life. More importantly, I expanded my cultural knowledge base and gained many new relatives—I now have sisters who are Kiowa, Crow and Potawatomi, and I have brothers who are Kickapoo, Quapaw and Comanche. In short, I understood and echoed the fond expression that I had first seen in my husband's eyes. Like thousands of other Native individuals who attended Haskell before me, I developed a deep appreciation for the institution that nurtured me.

As a Haskell student at the turn of the 21st century, the knowledge I had about the institution included some basic information, such as the date it was established and its general evolution from a boarding school to a four-year college, as well as knowledge of the "notables"—individuals such as Jim Thorpe and Billy Mills, who both attended Haskell early in their respective athletic careers. Additionally, I acquired other information through shared short stories or references made by instructors and students in the classroom, as well as informal gatherings. In other words, I had little bits and pieces of knowledge about the history of Haskell, and so I thought I knew something about the institution that had quickly captivated me, like it had so many before me. In spite of what I knew about Haskell, I would realize how small, how incredibly minute, those bits and pieces were when I was given an opportunity to research the institution further.

In the summer of 2002 I was hired as a museum technician at the Haskell Cultural Center and Museum to help produce a display of Haskell's history for the new museum. It was then that I first acquired my intense interest in the subject area that has led to the production of this text. Throughout my research on Haskell's history, it was the first two decades that I found most fascinating; after a tumultuous beginning with funding shortages, as well as turnover and inconsistency in the administration, the institution seemed to be flourishing, growing and improving to quickly become a flagship among its peers.

What became apparent very early in the research was the fact that the earliest students were exposed to extreme stress from the moment they arrived, and trauma was common in various aspects of their daily lives. After being forced to surrender all aspects of their own cultures, the students were then required to embrace competing aspects of a foreign culture. From the hard shoes and stiff, uniform clothes that replaced soft moccasins and buckskin or fabric clothes that often told stories about the wearer (i.e., what part of the country the student came from or how important the student was to relatives); to the human superiority complex that replaced the concept of interconnectedness between all things; to the Christian ideology that replaced traditional beliefs—there was an attempt made to completely erase students' prior life-ways and inculcate the standards, beliefs, traditions and culture of dominant society. This effort was summarized in the famous expression, coined by Captain Richard Pratt, "Kill the Indian and Save the Man."[2]

Meanwhile, the students were assigned to work in various areas of the institution for half of the day, performing tasks that kept the school running. For example, some male students worked the farm or constructed buildings, and girls were engaged in sewing school uniforms and doing the laundry of hundreds of students. At the same time, students were subject to external challenges. One of the first challenges faced during the first winter was a problem with heat in the buildings, an issue that would result in the first student deaths at the school. Sometimes it was inadequate food and/or medicine, and sometimes it was disease that traveled quickly in the overcrowded, ill-ventilated dorms. The bottom line is that the earliest students had it tough.[3]

On the other hand, what also became evident as my research on Haskell continued was the fact that in spite of the many sacrifices made by students (some willingly, some not), they found ways to survive. One clear example of survival can be found in the 1887 student petitions addressed to the Haskell superintendent and signed by students who were seeking to deal with student issues. These petitions, two in particular, are discussed later in this text. Perhaps it was the petitions, or more specifically, the student names on the petitions, that ignited my interest in the experiences of individuals and the stories of student connections. At any rate, as I continued to look through documents, certain student names became important; sometimes it was because they were repeated in other documents, and other times it was because of the information attached to the name. In either case, I often wondered about them: What are their stories and where are they told? The perimeters of the 2002 study did not allow me to answer those two questions in any depth, but I vowed to return to the subject at a later date, which in 2005–2006 I did as I focused on Haskell research for Ph.D. study.

As far as my portion of the Haskell history exhibit for the Haskell Cultural Center and Museum, ultimately, I was satisfied that I accomplished what I had set out to do in that particular project—I wanted people to feel as I did. I wanted them to feel sadness for the children who suffered, and I wanted them to feel rage for the realities that allowed such things to happen. But more importantly, I wanted them to know the collective strength of the students that emerged in the face of attempted cultural genocide, adversity, stress, and even death. I wanted them to feel the collective strength of the students that emerged from just the few stories that I was able to glean from the documents during my research. I wanted people to appreciate the fact that Haskell still exists today. I wanted them to know some of the stories of sacrifice and survival that I knew.

Altogether, the information contained within the following text tells a story of Haskell, of boarding schools, and of Indian education, as well as making some commentary, perhaps indirectly, on education in general in the late 19th century. It may be all that remains of a time and place long since gone, a vivid illustration of the challenges of historical research. It is an historical narrative that was constructed with pieces of text and words from the past that were found in a variety of primary and secondary sources. It is an interpretation of 19th century Haskell student experiences and events as seen through the eyes of one invested individual. It is a story of stories.

Respectfully, Theresa Milk
Lawrence, Kansas, 2007

PART I: FOUNDING OF AN INSTITUTION

Planning Years 1882–1884

In May of 1882, Congress appropriated money for the education of Native students at the three off-reservation boarding schools in existence at the time; additionally, funding for two new boarding schools was included. Dudley Chase Haskell, representative from the Second Congressional District in Kansas and chairman of the House Committee on Indian Affairs, advocated for one of the schools to be located in his hometown—Lawrence, Kansas. The government eventually agreed, with the stipulation that the city had to donate the land for the school.

The *Lawrence Daily Journal* responded to the federal government's challenge by devising a subscription fund. Lawrence merchants and citizens donated almost $10,000, which was used to purchase a 280-acre plot of land southeast of town. Construction began in August 1883. By July, 1884, there were three large limestone and pine buildings: the school building was in the middle, flanked by a girls' dormitory and a boys' dormitory on either side. Other smaller structures, such as barns and sheds, were constructed before the school officially opened in September, 1884.[4]

Haskell Superintendents 1884–1900

Dr. James Marvin was the first superintendent at Haskell when it officially opened in September, 1884. Marvin was a former Chancellor of the University of Kansas, and as a minister, he saw the inculcation of Christian morality as the primary focus of his work at Haskell. Beleaguered by failing health, institutional financial difficulties and bureaucracy, Marvin resigned in July 1885. His replacement, Colonel Arthur Grabowski, was a staunch military man who introduced rigor and discipline. In the process, he also alienated the local community, as well as the Native population. Grabowski was forced to resign in 1887.[5]

The third superintendent, former first Kansas Governor Charles Robinson, came aboard in early 1887. A prominent abolitionist and an experienced educator, Robinson reconnected the institution with both the local community and the Native population. Although the military rigor introduced by his predecessor remained in place for decades to come, Robinson's reign saw the introduction of the Haskell band, a school library and weekly socializing opportunities for the students—extra-curricular activities parallel to those in other mainstream educational institutions.[6]

Upon Robinson's retirement two years later, Colonel Oscar E. Learnard, the Lawrence businessman and attorney who sold the original 280-acre plot of land to the local citizens for the school, became the fourth superintendent, under protest. Learnard made it clear that he was only a temporary stand-in, and his replacement took the helm nine months later.[7]

Charles Meserve, an educator from Massachusetts, became superintendent in September, 1889. Like Robinson before him, Meserve believed in the capabilities of Native students. His desire to introduce a high school curriculum at Haskell was negated by the refusal of Congress to appropriate funding. However, Meserve would remain at Haskell for five years and provide a sense of stability during his tenure.[8]

In late 1894, John A. Swett, the assistant superintendent during Meserve's administration, became superintendent of Haskell, and with his administration came marked educational change. The five graded divisions were expanded to ten, and a kindergarten was introduced, in addition to a teacher training department and a business department.[9]

In 1898, Hervey B. Peairs, an Emporia State Normal School graduate who had been at various times teacher, principal and assistant superintendent at Haskell since his initial hire in 1887, was appointed superintendent, a position he would retain until 1910 when he was called to Washington. After a few years in D.C., Peairs would return to serve as Haskell's superintendent two more times prior to his retirement in 1931, making him the longest-serving superintendent in the school's history. In the meantime, the institution itself was evolving.[10]

The Evolution of the Institution

Initially, Haskell provided instruction in the grammar school grade levels of one through five, with an obvious focus on English-speaking skills. Three-and-one-half hours of each weekday were devoted to formal instruction and four hours were spent on industrial training, such as cooking, sewing, carpentry, masonry and farming. The course of study itself was "thoroughly" revised at the beginning of the 1894–95 school year to include a kindergarten and a normal (standard term for early teacher training schools) department. The kindergarten was touted as successful and "of great value as a model department" for the normal department. It is unclear exactly how many grade levels existed in addition to the kindergarten and normal classes at that point in the institutional history.[11]

A commercial department was introduced at the start of the 1895–96 school year. In addition to the commercial and normal departments and the kindergarten class, there were ten other grade levels as listed by Superintendent Swett in his annual report. They included: "chart class, first, second, third, and fourth primary; first, second, third, and fourth advanced; [and] senior grammar-school grade."[12]

In 1903, the commercial and normal departments were discontinued on the orders of Commissioner of Indian Affairs William Jones who wrote, "Commercial courses, normal courses, etc., have no place in the function of an Indian school." The business department was reopened in 1906, and the normal department was reestablished in 1921. It appears that both departments were discontinued prior to 1927 when Haskell was accredited as a high school by the State of Kansas. In 1935, a post-high school vocational program was established. The high school was phased out in 1962, and Haskell evolved into a post-high school vocational-technical institution. The last high school class graduated in 1965. A junior college curriculum was introduced in 1970, and the school's name was changed to Haskell Indian Junior College. It would become Haskell Indian Nations University in 1993 and begin offering baccalaureate programs in 1994.[13]

Haskell progressed rapidly during the first two decades, from five grade levels in 1884 to ten grades plus a kindergarten, as well as addition of the normal and commercial department in 1895. At the same time, students were engaged in daily industrial duties, but they were also increasingly exposed to various types of extra-curricular activities, as illustrated in a later section.

In addition to the expanding curriculum of 19th century Haskell, the institution grew rapidly from the original 280 acres of land with about 300 students in attendance at the end of 1884. By 1891, the school had expanded to 650 acres of land with an average attendance of 514 students. In 1901, the average attendance of students was listed as 655. It is unclear if the land base had also grown at that point.[14]

It was my exposure to existing historical narratives about the institution that led to my curiosity about some of the 19th century Haskell students: "What are their stories and where are they told?" Those two questions began this particular adventure into historical inquiry. Ultimately, by utilizing the limited evidence and operating within my understanding of the historical research process, I have been able to construct stories that allow insight into student experiences at 19th century Haskell.

Collecting the pieces of these stories has been both a challenge and an adventure. There is little evidence to construct stories of the lives of most people from the 19th century. It is even more difficult in the case of students who were dependent, disciplined, counted and classified, and had no rights. It is no less challenging when looking at the lives of Haskell students. However, with the information found in a handful of letters, a newspaper, and a long buried document, I have found fragmentary stories of 19th century Haskell students. Of course, my inferences may be flawed and the interpretation could be biased, but in the end, this story of stories adds to the history of Haskell.

Various authors, including Adams (1995), Anderson (1997) and Vuckovic (2001), have described in detail some of the harsh realities of 19th century Haskell. From the initial assault on the student, including the stripping away of names, languages, traditional clothing and religious practices, to the various hardships the students were subject to such as separation from family, military discipline, sickness and malnutrition, Native students at Haskell in the late 1800s were forced to abandon all that they knew and replace it with "civilized" behaviors and knowledge.

In other words, the students had to sacrifice. Some sacrificed more than others, but they all had to sacrifice some part of themselves. For some it was their name, their identity. For many the sacrifice was in being separated from their families for years. And for a few it was their health, a limb or their life. In some manner, all of the students at Haskell in the 19th century sacrificed. What follows are stories of some of those who sacrificed. They offer one a glimpse of the human anguish that this experience entailed. In doing so, they provide another dimension to the history of the institution, boarding schools, Indian education and even late 19th century American society in general terms. With that said, I turn my attention to the stories themselves.

PART II: STORIES OF STUDENT SACRIFICE

The First Students at Haskell

The very first students did not necessarily start off their "educational process" in the same way as the students that followed. Prior to the official opening of Haskell, a number of young Native men were brought in to prepare the school for students. The available information on each of the men varies: Dan Blue Jacket, a 17-year old Shawnee, arrived at Haskell on February 15, 1884. It appears he may have been brought in as a carpenter to assist the hired non-Native farmer. Dan would stay until March of 1886 when, for reasons unknown, he was "sent home by Inspector." Whitt Matthews, a 17-year-old Arapahoe, arrived on July 19, 1884. He would stay until his three-year term expired on October 18, 1887. Although it is not noted, it would be logical to conclude that Whitt was the assistant farmer referred to in some of the texts.[15]

On May 13, 1884, government officials transferred six young men from Chilocco, a boarding school in Oklahoma. A seventh, Alex Peters, arrived on July 14, 1884, also from Chilocco. There are two separate entries in the *Registration Record of Haskell Institute, 1884–1889* ledger for each of those, and I have come to call them "the Chilocco seven." All seven are listed together early in the book under the title "Record of Pupils transferred from Chilocco Ind. School, Indian Territory," which includes their tribal origins and blood, as well as a notation that they are all "physically sound."

There is also something written in the "remarks" column of the document for each of the seven. There is a detailed entry made in two of the cases: Colonel Horn, who was "Employed as Teamster July 1st 84" and then "Employed as Irregular Laborer at $25.00 per month from May 13" (year not noted); and Alex Peters, who was "Employed as an Irregular laborer," then "appointed as 2nd assistant farmer on Sept 1, 84." Additionally, he was "A graduate of Hampton Va." (The words were indeed underlined and double underlined in the actual text.) The entries in the remarks section of the other five say simply, "returned to Chilocco Sept 1, 84." Upon further investigation, I found that most of them didn't actually return to Chilocco; in fact, it appears that most, if not all, of the Chilocco seven stayed on to become students at Haskell.

In a later section of the 1884–1889 registration record, the document shifts from the original format of recording students by tribes and arrival dates to an alphabetical listing of students from 1884–1889. Each of the Chilocco seven has another entry in the latter portion of the text. With the exception of Frank Carter and Alex Peters, it adds a little more information to the student's record:

* ❖ Frank Carter was Sac & Fox, age unknown
* ❖ Colonel Horn, a 17-yr-old Cheyenne, completed his first three-year term, "entered for a second term of two years Sept. 1887," and stayed until his second term expired on June 30, 1889
* ❖ Owen Honancheko, Kiowa, age unknown, stayed until April 5, 1887, when he was "sent home sick"
* ❖ Alex Peters, was a 20-year-old Menominee
* ❖ Rush Roberts, Pawnee, age unknown, was designated an assistant farmer on July 1, 1884
* ❖ Pearlie Whitmore, an 18-year-old Comanche, "deserted" on October 1, 1886
* ❖ Coemet Wood, Caddo, was 19 when he arrived. He stayed until his term expired on June 30, 1887[16]

It is important to note the detailed information provided for these young men; this clarifies the vague prior references made regarding this group of individuals.

In his 1936 text, Ames, in talking about the opening enrollment, states, "Seven boys had earlier been transferred from another new school, at Chilocco, Oklahoma, to work on the Lawrence school farm through the spring and summer, and these were in the entering class . . . "; he makes no mention of the other two Native men, although he notes, "a school farmer was engaged early in the year and with the help of a few Indian boys, there was begun the history of the Haskell farm." Granzer (1937) does mention "a farmer and a carpenter [who] began service in March, 1884," and the "six Indian boys who had been transferred from Chilocco in the spring" to help "the farmer and an assistant." However, the role played by the young men in helping to create the exterior grounds and physical attributes of the Institute is minimized by Granzer, as it was with Ames.[17]

Anderson (1997) and Vuckovic (2001) both detail the extent of the labor produced by this group: these young Native men, under the direction of the hired farmer, planted and fenced 80 acres of crops; fenced 200 acres of grazing land; planted 400 fruit trees; prepared a large vegetable garden; transported supplies from the railroad depot to the institution; removed debris from the grounds; graded the excess earth around the buildings; cleaned and prepared dormitories, store-rooms and school-rooms; and constructed kitchen pantries and tables for dining halls. In spite of the acknowledgement of their labors, both authors continue to refer to the Chilocco group as "Indian boys" who came to assist the farmer, the farmer's assistant, and a carpenter in pre-paring the school grounds. Further investigation of this group of nine leads me to the realization that all but the farmer himself were Native and from the available information, it appears that all were young Na-tive men, not "Indian boys" as previously stated. Perhaps a part of their sacrifice was to work in relative anonymity.[18]

In the historical narratives on Haskell, the first group of students is presented as twenty-two individuals who were present at the offi-cial opening ceremony on September 17, 1884. Most of the sources are consistent in presenting the information that twelve Ponca males arrived on September 1 and eight Chippewa and Muncie children (five females and three males) arrived on the sixteenth, one day before the opening. The remaining two students are referred to as "boys" or "farm boys," if they are mentioned at all. It is unclear where the infor-mation originates, but that is the extent of the information presented in any of the secondary sources to date.

Now, with the ledger, it is possible to clarify and expand slightly on this part of the school's history. For example, the ledger notes that there were twelve Ponca boys and men who arrived at Haskell on August 30, 1884; they ranged in age from eleven to twenty-four. And the group of eight Chippewa and Muncie children, five female and three male, did arrive on September 16; their age ranges were nine to fourteen and twelve to eighteen, respectively. Indeed, there is now more information available on the individuals who are listed by all other sources as the first students at Haskell; however, I will leave that topic exploration for another researcher. I have already given my interpretation of the subject. I see the nine young men I introduced earlier as the first group of students at Haskell. With that, I now turn my discussion to other aspects of 19th century Haskell history.[19]

The First Decade

The first ten years of Haskell were focused on "civilization" of Native students. Education included basic English, reading, and writing skills in grades one through five; and Christianity, citizenship, and manual labor. For four hours each day, the Native student was engaged in industrial work, and three or four hours were spent in formal academic instruction.

The students at Haskell in the early years suffered the most. First of all, their method and mode of arrival at the institution were not always pleasant. At all boarding schools at various points in time and to different degrees, children were forcibly removed from their homes; parents were coerced and threatened with the withholding of rations, essentially starvation; or parents were forced to choose between children in order to keep the rest of the family alive—they would have to pick one child to send to boarding school to keep receiving their rations.[20]

As grim as the reality could be, there were certainly Native parents who saw the boarding schools as an opportunity they wished for their children. For example, Mrs. Margaret Bedell wrote a letter to Superintendent Robinson dated June 17, 1888:

Dear Sir:
Your favor of 9th visit [?] with contents Postage Stamps for fare

of Mary Ann Coon. I sent her on Tuesday morning and hope she arrived at the Institute all right. I wish her to remain at School during vacation and do not wish her to work out during that time, (As I heard that was allowed if the pupil desired to). I do not wish her to go out in town alone or have any correspondence, or any intimate relations with the male scholars. Any correspondence not from me, I should be pleased if you will forward it to me — My greatest desire is for her to learn and upon the expiration of the three years she may be an ornament in society — Yours Truly   Mrs. Margaret Bedell Topeka, KS

(P.S.) Of course I would like to hear occasionally how she progresses. And if she appears content. She not knowing how to write I will have to be patient until she learns.[21]

It can be assumed that the letter was written by the mother of the young woman—especially considering the references made regarding contact with male "scholars."

The use of the words "scholars" and "an ornament in society" illustrate the expectations of the letter writer for the education to be provided to her offspring. It also gives some indication of the mother's own educational level. Interestingly, there is no entry in the 1884–1889 official registration book for Mary Ann Coon, nor is there an entry with Margaret Bedell listed as parent. Furthermore, there is no student file in the federal archives for Mary Ann Coon.

Sometimes parents had other reasons for wanting their children to stay at Haskell. The half-Potawatomi brothers William and George Pearce were 17 and 15 years old, respectively, when they arrived at Haskell on July 9, 1887. Eleven months later, in June of 1888, Superintendent Robinson received this letter from Wichita, Kansas:

Sir:

I received a letter from Willie wishing to come home now at present I would rather the boys would remain at the school as this is a hard place for boys and times are dull and their mother is in poor health this summer and it would be better if they could make us a short visit in cold weather. Please explain this to them Thanking you for the care you have taken of my sons I remain

    Yours Respectfully

    /s/Chris Pearce

Like some parents, Mr. Pearce saw Haskell as a better place for his children than the hardships of home. Incidentally, William was allowed seven days furlough, one year later, on July 7, 1889; George departed on July 16, 1889 for eight days furlough. One must wonder why the brothers were not allowed furlough at the same time. It appears that not only did the institution separate siblings at school in the early years, but sometimes the administration worked to separate siblings at home, too. In any case, according to their student files, the brothers did return to Haskell after their furloughs, but they apparently decided not to finish the term. William was "released" on March 17, 1890, and George "deserted" on March 31, 1890. Perhaps William got into trouble and was "released" as a result. Meanwhile, George may have been stewing over the matter and eventually decided he did not want to stay at Haskell if his brother was not there, so he left.[22]

Some parents who sent their children to Haskell were disillusioned upon the return of their offspring. Consider the following letter written by a student to one of the instructors at Haskell:

    Pawnee Agency, Ind Terr

      Oct 16th, 1887

    Dear Miss Smith

    I now taken pleasure in writing to you. I was glad to get you letter. But I am sorry that I can not come back again. I have been asking and asking father to let me go back and stay two more years but he is not willing to let me go. I want to go so bad because I had promised Gov. that I was coming back to Haskell so did my father said that I can go back. But after I came home he ask me what I have learne [sic] while I was at

Haskell I told him that I have learn to sew and so he when to the Supt and ask him if he can give me a please at school and so he ask me what did I do when I was at Haskell I told him that I was sew so they put me to sew at school. Miss Smith the seamstress always ask me what you do I tell her every thing what you do and then she said it was nice we will do that. But oh how I love to see Grandmother this very minte [sic]. I often think about you's and her what a nice time I use to have when I go visit to Grandmother. Yet I have a nice time in ride on the horse back with me cousin Mollie. Miss Smith one day I was cry because my father is not willing to let me go again. Seamstress came to me and said to me Gertie I want you's to love me as well as you did to Miss Smith I'll be good to you so that you wont want to go back to Haskell. But I can not love her as I do to you and grandmas. Tell Mrs. Luddington I send my best love her. Tell Rose Carrie and Lola that I send my love to them I like to see them. I have something to tell you my sister's has a little baby boy she give it to me so I made two little drases for him. Miss Lizzie Smith Emily is dead she died week ago on Wednesday but she died in a quite way. We are all well just now. John Brown's wife has a baby. Tell Gov. I send my love to him and all of the other emple and children. This is Sunday how I wish I could go to church and hear preacher take or go to Sunday school in afternoon to Miss Batsford class. The reason I want to go back to Haskell because I want to go to school and learne more here I don't go to school I only sew. James Murie has a good wife have nice home. Smith Mr. Weeks married Annie Gillingham sister after he came home from Haskell. I haven't see her yet but I will ask her how much you have to pay for it and then I'll tell you. Josiah Patterson came home after Emily had died. James Bishop is well and happy. I would be glad and happy if I should see Haskell again. Miss Smith I was not lonesome when Mr. Pears [sic] came so I didn't want to go back I though I would stay here little long and ask father if I could go back when I got lonesome so I did ask father and he no I should not go. Write soon I am always glad to get letter from Haskell. I will my letter and will try to be a good girl

Gertie Wilde

Pawnee Agency   Ind Territory

P.S. give this other one to Josie and Gertrude Miss Smith

This lengthy letter provides a wealth of information about the community aspects of Haskell, and this is why it is helpful to present it here in its entirety. First of all, Gertie's fondness for the teacher is obvious. In fact, Gertie was fond of a number of individuals at Haskell; she expresses her warm feelings about students, teachers and others. Additional research has actually allowed some of the individuals in this letter to be further identified.[23]

In the employee list filed with the 1887 Haskell superintendent's annual report, Miss Lizzie Smith is listed as a seamstress who was hired on July 1, 1885; Lizzie's name continues to show up on the employee lists through 1889. There is a gap here, as the annual reports for 1890 were not available during this research. In the end, Lizzie's name does not show up on the lists from 1891 on; instead, the seamstress is Anna Fischer.[24]

Miss Batsford is surely Della Botsford, a teacher who was hired on October 15, 1886. Interestingly, like Lizzie, Della's name shows up on the employee lists through 1889, but not on the lists from 1891 on. I would think that perhaps Mrs. Luddington is a teacher; however, there is no name even similar included on the employee lists, so it is unclear what connection she had to Haskell and Gertie. One very intriguing aspect of the letter is Gertie's reference to "Grandmother" or "grandmas," so I wonder to whom is she referring? It was someone Gertie loved and visited, as noted in the letter, and she was obviously connected to Haskell or she would not be mentioned in the letter. In any case, it is apparent that Gertie had fond memories of all of these individuals who were both instructors and students at the institution. The letter also conveys a sense of community. Through the letter, a former student is keeping a teacher informed about other former students, and so the Haskell community remained connected to its students and vice versa, a role *The Indian Leader* would play after its 1897 beginning. Gertie's story might have ended there were it not for the ledger book. The information provided in the ledger not only allows us to learn more about Gertie, but it also supplies us with information about some of the other individuals mentioned in the letter. Between the letter and the ledger, fragmented stories of 19th century Haskell students begin to emerge. I will explore those stories to some degree, but first, it is helpful to introduce the letter writer.

Gertie Wilde, a full-blood Pawnee, was sixteen years old when she arrived at Haskell on September 19, 1884. She apparently stayed until her term expired in August 1887. Gertie arrived at Haskell with a Pawnee name, *Tsta-ha-ta*; but when she left Haskell, she had an English name, new acquaintances and a fondness for the institution and all that it held. It is worth noting here that the ledger lists Gertie as "Re-entered Aug. 22, 1888," so, ultimately, she got her wish to return. There is no further information available on Gertie; however, the limited registration information, combined with the letter, provide us with a small picture of one young woman who was a student at 19th century Haskell. Additionally, Gertie's letter provides bits and pieces of the lives of other students of the same era.

When Gertie arrived at Haskell on September 19, 1884, she came with a group of twenty-one full-blooded Pawnee youths ranging in age from thirteen to twenty-three. The group was composed of nineteen males and two females. Some of the names are familiar. John Brown, James Murie, Josiah Patterson and James Bishop, each referred to in the letter, were all in Gertie's group of Pawnee students. The information available on each of them varies.

John Brown, one of the oldest in the group at twenty-three, arrived at Haskell with the name *Ke-wa-koo*. It is unclear how long he stayed, but we do know he was "Sent home." It is also noted in the ledger that John was "Too old and sick," which is probably a reference to the reason he was sent home from the institution. Apparently John Brown was not in very bad shape, for he returned home, married and his wife "has a baby" according to Gertie.

James Bishop, or *Rah-tah-tuts-ke-pe-se-soo*, was twenty-one years old when he arrived. He stayed until July 1, 1887 when his term expired. Apparently, he returned home to Indian Territory where he was "well and happy."

James Murie, or *Young Eagle*, was also twenty-one upon his arrival at Haskell. There is no further information in the ledger on him, but the name James R. Murie does show up on the 1886 employee list under the position of "Assistant disciplinarian." The dates of employment are listed as July 1, 1885, to May 31, 1886. The name does not show up on any of the future employee lists. Apparently, James was a student at Haskell who was employed at the institution during his second year there. Then James went back to Indian Territory and found himself "a good wife have nice home" (quoting the letter).

Josiah Patterson is the fourth of the male students Gertie refers to in her letter; there is more information available on Josiah than on the other three. In fact, to some degree, his story is longer than most un-covered to this point. His story at Haskell begins as follows: Josiah or *Ah-cah-she*, a full-blood Pawnee, was sixteen when he arrived on September 19, 1884. According to the ledger, Josiah finished out his first four-year term in July 1888 and "Reentered for two years" on August 22, 1888; he then went to Silver Lake, Kansas, on "5 days furlough" on July 11, 1889. There is no further information available in the ledger on Josiah; however, there is more to his story.

In early May, 1888, Josiah, along with eighteen other male Haskell students, put his signature to a petition requesting accountability from administration, an incident that is explored later in this text. Two months later, Josiah wrote a letter to Superintendent Robinson af-ter he went home following his first term. The letter reads as follows, quoted in his original language without change:

Write to me soon please
Pawnee Agency Ind. Terr. July 6th 1888
My dear Chas. Robinson
I though I write to you few line I am very glad to get home now. I can tell you. go to Haskell I not I to know. my folks are

well and brothers & Sisters too. Gov Robinson I guess you to
want me any moor. if you want me and write to soon please.
well how Miss Campbell getting along this time. tell Miss
Campbell his are well.

Josiah Patterson

Obviously, Josiah was still working on the basics of the English language; however, it appears that although he was "glad to get home,"
he was also eager to return to Haskell. According to the registration
information, Josiah's wish to return to the school was granted later that
same summer. It is unclear exactly how long or if he stayed at Haskell
past August 1890, which would have been the end of his second term.
What is clear, however, is the fact that there is one tombstone in the
cemetery that reads: Josiah Patterson, 1868–1893.[25]

As a final note to this story, it is interesting that Josiah's ledger entry
indicates that he did not go home until July 2, 1888, after the end of
his first term and yet Gertie's letter was written in late 1887, and she
mentions Josiah going home "after Emily had died." This is a concrete
example of the some of the inconsistencies to be found in the information presented in the ledger. However, in spite of the discrepancies,
each little piece of information has some value, even if questionable.
In any case, there is one final student to discuss who is drawn out of
Gertie's letter.

In the Pawnee group, Gertie was one of two females. The other
was Emily Bayhylle, or *Sta-pe-l-lo,* who was nineteen at the time she
entered Haskell. Her ledger entry states: "Went home Nov. 12, 86; apt
seamstress at Pawnee Agency; Returned Mar 6, 87. Sent home June
29, 87 sick." Emily Bayhylle's name also shows up on an employee list;
in 1887; she is listed as an assistant laundress who was employed from
Mar. 9, 1887, to June 30, 1887. It is reasonable to conclude that this
is the same Emily mentioned in Gertie's letter. It appears that Emily
was one of the students who went home sick only to succumb shortly
thereafter. Perhaps that was her sacrifice. In the end, Gertie's letter has
provided us with additional bits of information on at least five other
19th century Haskell students. And now we know the ultimate fate of

at least one early Haskell student, Emily Bayhylle. With that said, I turn to another aspect of early boarding school life—identity destruction.

Destruction of Identity

Upon arrival at a boarding school institution, students were stripped of their language, dress, spiritual beliefs, societal norms and culture. Any cultural items in a child's possession were confiscated, and the students were subjected to punishment for offenses including speaking their language. In many cases, Native youth were stripped of their names; they were stripped of all aspects of their existing identity.

Some authors have discussed the issue of identity destruction, or the stripping away of one's name, in the boarding schools in general, as well as specifically at Haskell. However, the information shared is scant; in most cases, authors introduce a few of the most outrageous cases of Native students burdened with a foreign white name by mere mention of the names. It is my intent to expand on this issue slightly by utilizing information found in the 1884–1889 student registration ledger.

The following table is information taken from the ledger; it provides the details available on historical names.

Based on the information in Table 1, the process of naming students after historical or literary figures was not restricted to one incidence. As shown by the dates, it happened sporadically throughout the five years, so it was indeed somewhat of a common practice during the early boarding school days, as mentioned by other authors. Although the range of Indian names, pronunciations and translation issues point to the need for school personnel to find a workable moniker, it is still a mystery why school personnel chose to give some students these types of names. It is possible that it was to help students identify with "great men" in the dominant culture, to aid in assimilation. Perhaps that is the case, but it seems potentially cruel in retrospect.

Table 1
Selected students from 1884–1889 Haskell Student Registration Ledger, Haskell Cultural Center & Museum Archives

Arrival Date	Name	Tribe Degree	Age	Indian Name	Parent	Departure Date Reason	General Notes
Sept. 19, 1884	Julius Caesar	Pawnee Full	16	*Sah we ta*	Julius Caesar		
Sept. 19, 1884	Henry W. Beecher	Pawnee Full	18			July '87 Term expired	Reentered for second term Sept. 20 '87 Sent home sick July 9, 1888
Sept. 21, 1884	Horace Greeley	Arapahoe Full	17				
Oct. 8, 1884	William Penn	Osage Full	11	*Kah he gra in kah*	William Penn	March 15, 1887 Deserted	
Dec. 9, 1884	James Hamilton	Cheyenne Full	20	*Hawk walk*	Elk Horn	July 11, 89 Term expired	Entered for a second term of two years
Dec. 15, 1884	Grover Cleveland	Cheyenne Full	14	Illegible name	Illegible name		
Dec. 24, 1884	Robinson Cruisoe	Shawnee Full	11		Delaware Robinson		
Jan. 3, 188?	Napoleon Bonaparte	Shawnee ?	13		Sam Wilson		
Nov. 26, 1885 Jan. 6, 1885	Andrew Jackson	Osage Half	18	*Mon kah*	Meh pah hah	Oct. 10, 1887 Deserted	
Sept. 2, 1888	Charles Robinson	Cheyenne Full	18	*Mexican Red Skin*		Oct. 13, 1888 Deserted	
Feb. 11, 1889	Oscar Learnard	Wichita Full	20	*Tar har no*	Jim ? (Chief)	March 9, 1889 Deserted	Arrested by City Marshall at Walton? KS brought back Mar. 17, 1889

It was hard enough for an adolescent to have to adjust to a new name and a new identity, but the further hardship faced by the student who would eventually discover that his new name was tied to an alien identity that he would learn about through a book is possibly immeasurable. No wonder William Penn and Andrew Jackson "deserted"; their new identities offered few reasons to stay.

As for Charles Robinson and Oscar Learnard, it seems that at the ages of 18 and 20, it would be extremely difficult to trade a name with meaning at home for one that belonged to a white man who had very recently been a superintendent at the school. I can be certain that the two young Native men did not see the honor bestowed in the names they were given; perhaps that is why they both "deserted" within six weeks of their naming.

As a final note on this issue, it is unclear why Andrew Jackson has two arrival dates. There are a number of like instances in the registration book where one individual has two dates listed. However, there is no indication of the reason. Interestingly, when I examined various students' files, there were two Grover Cleveland and three Andrew Jackson files. The two Grover Cleveland(s) apparently arrived on August 20, 1898 from Fort Defiance, Arizona: one was a 17-year-old Apache and the other a 14-year-old Navajo. Neither the arrival date nor the tribal affiliation of either of these students is consistent with the information given in the ledger about the 1884 Grover Cleveland, and there are no more Grover Cleveland student files in the federal archives. What happened to the fourteen-year-old, full-blood Cheyenne named Grover Cleveland? Did he just disappear? This seems to be a case of a forgotten child.

In the case of Andrew Jackson, there is a student file that corresponds with the information in the ledger. Unlike most of the student files viewed, the information on the typewritten, one-page paper inside one Andrew Jackson's folder is the same as the information hand-written on the ledger. The second Andrew Jackson, an eleven-year-old Seneca, arrived on September 1, 1887, from Wyandotte City, Indian Territory. His file contains more information than the first one about the student's comings and goings. The third Andrew Jackson was a nineteen-year-old, full-blood Pima who arrived from Sacaton, Arizona, on August 10, 1907. In any case, my attention now turns from various students who were victims of identity destruction and for whom there is no further information available and to one student who has a somewhat more complete story.[26]

Mary Riley—Teacher? Student? Both?

Because there are so few primary documents from Haskell in the 1800s that have survived, it is, of course, a challenge to present an adequate representation of any one individual at any point in time. It is therefore not the intent of this study to present itself as an absolutely complete account of the time, yet there is, nonetheless, value to be found in the small tidbits and pieces that form a glimpse of the 1800s Haskell student perspective.

On the other hand, it must be acknowledged that the accuracy of the available documents is also in question in many instances; therefore, obvious inaccuracies are noted. However, there is no need to discount the entire record due to the errors, intended or not, found within a document. With that in mind, the following story illustrates how, in the official records, sometimes the line blurs between student and employee. The story illustrates one example of an extreme case of apparent misrepresentation of an individual that can be found in the available records. It is the story of one young woman by the name of Mary Riley.

Mary Riley is listed in the 1884–1889 Haskell student registration ledger. Her entry has little information; she was listed as full-blood Seminole, and seventeen years old when she arrived on August 17, 1888. There is no information listed in the pupil address, parent name, or parent address categories; however, there is one more entry—"Died Oct. 7, 88." In the Haskell Cemetery there is a tombstone that reads: Mary Riley, Seminole, 1871–1888. This might have been the beginning and end of Mary's story, but research illustrates that her story is more complex and confusing than just a cursory examination would indicate.[27]

In Charles Robinson's collection of letters there are three separate letters from two consecutive summers that have the beautiful penmanship and signature of "Mary Riley." A careful study of the forming of some of the dominant letters and characters leaves no doubt that all three letters were written by the same individual.

The first letter, in its entirety, reads as follows:

512 N. 25th St. Omaha, Neb.

July 21st 1887

Supt. Robinson

Dear Sir;

I am enjoying my vacation and hope to return by the 1st of August or earlier if required. We have had intense heat but hope you have not suffered from it. Hoping you are all well, with kindest regard to Mrs. Robinson.

Yours Respectfully

Mary Riley.

Obviously, this Mary Riley was at Haskell in 1887, a year prior to the one listed as a student on the ledger. Additionally, the tone of the letter does not seem to be indicative of a student. The following summer, Superintendent Robinson received another letter from Mary Riley:

Morrisonville. Clinton Co. N.Y.

July 3rd, 1888.

Dear Governor Robinson,

My journey home was very pleasant being cool. I find all well and happy. I am now surrounded by my Eastern friends but my thoughts turn to those who have been so kind to me in the West. I hope you are all well.

Brother John sends kind regards to you.

With best wishes to Mrs. Robinson.

Yours Respectfully,

Mary Riley

This letter makes Mary's story even more puzzling. First of all, the first letter came from Omaha, Nebraska, while this one comes from New York. At the same time, there is a familiarity about it that would indicate that Mary Riley was writing to an acquaintance as opposed to an authority figure. Additionally, there is the reference to Brother John — is that her brother or a man of the cloth?

Less than two weeks later, Mary Riley sent another letter to Superintendent Robinson:

Plattsburgh, N.Y.
July 15, 1888
Hon. G. Robinson Supt, Haskell Institute
Dear Sir.

Your letter of the 7th inst. Enclosing check for balance of amount left in your hands for my board is received for which you have my thanks. I would like to have my leave of absence extended to about the middle of August if it can be done without inconvenience. I will however return Aug 1st, if you desire it and will so advise me.

My brother hopes for great improvement in the schools from the change in the law placing them under the management of a separate Bureau.

He wishes to be kindly remembered.

Yours truly,
Mary Riley
P.S. Address me at Morrisonville N.Y.
[handwritten note on corner of letter—Ans. July 25]

The third letter tends to clarify the emerging impression that Mary Riley was, in fact, a teacher at Haskell Institute. The discussion of her brother's opinion illustrates political awareness, even if only his, an indication of "culture" or "education." Furthermore, she uses the phrase "leave of absence." Ultimately, based on the presentation to be found in the letters—the penmanship, language and writing skills—it appears that Mary Riley was a teacher.[28]

This view is bolstered when the Haskell Institute employee listing that was filed with the Annual Report is considered. Mary Riley is listed as a Teacher for three years beginning in 1887. According to the 1887 list, Mary's term of service for the fiscal year was September 17, 1886, to June 30, 1887, at a salary per annum of $600, of which she was actually paid $472.83. She was paid the entire $600 in the following year, and her term of service is listed as July 1, 1887, to June 30, 1888. Furthermore, the name Mary Riley shows up again on the 1889 Haskell employee list with a term of service from July1888 to June1889. However, the name does not show up in future lists.[29]

So if Mary Riley was a teacher, why is her name included in the student registration list? Perhaps it was to bolster the student numbers, which would explain why there is so little information tied to her name. Or it could be that a female student arrived who was given Mary Riley's name, but it seems that if that were the case there would be more information attached to the student entry, such as an Indian name that required the change. Most likely, the former scenario was the reality—Mary Riley was listed to increase the student count, but still a question remains—Why is there a tombstone at Haskell with the name Mary Riley on it? If there was only one Mary Riley who was a teacher, why did she end up in the Haskell cemetery? It seems that if Mary Riley was an employee and was being paid, then there would be money available to send her body home to her brother John.

Another question to consider is the "Seminole" designation on the tombstone. Was Mary Riley, the teacher, a Seminole? Perhaps it is worth noting that it appears that Mary Riley, the student, did not arrive alone at Haskell. Her ledger entry is listed below that of another Seminole, Orrin Red Field, a thirteen-year-old who also arrived on August 17, 1888. Like Mary's, Orrin's student entry is devoid of details outside of what has already been stated.[30]

It is possible that Mary was indeed a Seminole who was educated in Eastern schools and arrived at Haskell as a teacher, perhaps bringing a fellow Seminole with her on her return to Haskell in the fall of 1888. She may have then been listed in the student registration, because she was a Native, to bolster the enrollment. And she may have been buried here for convenience. What are the alternatives? The interpretation is left to the reader. In the end, this shows the uncertainty of ascertaining the identity of students in this era. In any case, I now move my discussion beyond identity to student health.

Health Issues

Various authors have done an adequate job of detailing some of the various health and welfare issues faced by the students of the early boarding schools and Haskell. According to Child (1998), "Communicable diseases flourished in the Indian boarding schools . . . The boarding school setting was an atmosphere conducive to the spread of disease." As with the other boarding schools, outbreaks of sickness—including respiratory infections, pneumonia, diphtheria, trachoma, scrofula and tuberculosis—at Haskell were commonplace. Contributing factors included overcrowding, inadequate food, "an often underpaid staff (who) provided irregular medical care," not to mention the "apathetic boarding school officials (who) frequently failed to heed their own directions calling for the segregation of children in poor health from the rest of the student body." Sickness was a harsh reality of boarding school life, and it was no different at Haskell.[31]

Anderson (1997) and Vuckovic (2001) have done an admirable job of vividly portraying many of the health and welfare issues faced by the early Haskell students. Therefore, this text does not delve too deeply into those questions. However, it is important to note that because they were often provided with inadequate food, shelter, clothing and/or medical attention and subjected to strict discipline and hard labor, many students did not make it through their initial term. Some deserted and were never heard from again; some were sent home sick, only to succumb to illness shortly after their arrival at home; some never made it home at all—they remain buried here; and some just disappeared. There is no way to measure the total numbers of students in any of those categories, but the ledger does provide some clues. For the most part, however, there are no records to absolutely prove these types of things happened and to what extent, but we do know they happened.

Charles Campbell was an eighteen-year-old Arapahoe who had arrived at Haskell on November 12, 1885, from Darlington, Indian Territory. Although little is known about Charles, there is a letter written to his father that provides one with some sense of the young man's plight:

March 14, 1888
Dear Father
I thought I would like to write to you this afternoon and I hope you will be glad to hear from me this time. I want to tell you about me and I got sore my neck along ago about one month and I am sorry all time because I don't like sore my neck. And I like to hear from you this time because you never write to me. What is the matter with you and because I want you write to me very soon because I like to hear from you. Please tell me how are you getting along this spring I should like to know very much if you write to me. I glad. I like to go home this summer because I can stay here this school because I got sore my neck this spring. I want ask you some money. Please you sent to me money and some moccasins because I like some money and some moccasins too. I tell you about my Lesson third reader and Geography and Arithmetic and Language and Spelling. And all my lesson of difference words. And I trying hard to learn all every thing this month. Well I guess stop writing letter for this time because I have nothing to say I think this is all
    From you son Charles G Campbell
    Answer very soon if you please.
    Cheyenne Arapahoe Agency
    Darlington Indian Territory[32]

Based on this letter, we know Charles was sick and we know that he hadn't had contact with his father recently. We also know that Charles was eager to share with his father what he was learning—perhaps he was seeking to please his father with his enthusiasm for education—hence his references to different subjects.[33]

Because this letter is in the Superintendent's file as a single piece, it would appear that the original letter was intercepted, never to be received by its intended recipient. In the end, Charles Campbell's name appeared on the sick list compiled by the Haskell physician on May 25, 1888; his illness is listed as scrofula. That would explain the comments Charles made about his sore neck. Scrofula is considered a tuberculous infection of the skin of the neck. It is unclear what ever became of Charles Campbell. His student file reads: "Dropped: May 26, 1888," one day after his sickness was defined. There is no further information available on Charles Campbell. There is no tombstone in the school cemetery with his name on it. I cannot help but wonder, is he another forgotten one? Ultimately, his sacrifice is clear. He fell victim to one of the forms of sickness that ravaged Haskell from time to time. In other words, his sacrifice was his health. Ultimately, Charles wanted to go home, but it would appear he did not get his wish. He was not alone.[34]

Can I Please Go Home?

In the beginning, students were required to stay at Haskell for a three- or four-year term, during which time they were not allowed to go home. It appeared at first that the younger children were kept for four years, while some of the older students were allowed to go home for the summer after three years. However, based on the findings in the ledger, it is now unclear what the perimeters were for either length of stay, although it does appear that following their first term, students could return for a second term that lasted two years.

The initial lengthy separation of the students from their families was certainly difficult for both the Native parents and the students. Naturally, sometimes the students just wanted to go home for a short visit, so they would appeal to the Superintendent. Elsie Davis, a full-blood Cheyenne, had arrived on September 19, 1884; she wanted to go home after three-and-a-half years, so she appealed to Superintendent Robinson:

March 9, 1888

To Gov Chas Robinson.

I thought I would write to you. I am going to tell you that my father is sick and my sister wants me to go home. I am in room number 3 I go to school all day. I am going to ask you if it should be right for me to go home. One of my brother's are going to get married at Carlisle. They are going to live in Philadelphia in West Grove. If I go home I would come back. I have been here three years an a half.

From Elsie Davis.

Ten years old

Obviously, Elsie was looking for any and every reason to go home; one can assume that the administration thought, as seems evident, that her tone did not ring of necessity, but more of desire.[35]

Rarely were the requests of parents or students granted if the term was not up. In Elsie's case, the superintendent received a letter four months later, dated July 11, 1888, written on behalf of "a few parents who want their children to come home for vacation ... Poor old man [illegible] Bull Bear wanted to know if his daughter Elias [sic] Davis come home." Based on the information in the Elsie Davis entry in the 1884–1889 student ledger, notably "Bull Bear" listed as parent, it is apparent that this is the same young lady. Although she didn't get to go home when she initially asked, Elsie departed from Haskell on July 19, 1888, after her "term expired." As promised, she returned to Haskell for a second term on November 29, 1888; however, it is unclear how long she stayed or what happened to her.[36]

During the first two decades, for the most part, the only reason students went home before their terms were up was because of sickness. However, there may have been exceptions to the rule. Consider the last request of a dying man—he asks to see his children one more time.

Ottawa, Kan, Feb. 20th, 1888

Ex. Gov. C. Robinson

Sup. Haskell Institute

Dear Sir: Mr. Edward McCoonse is very sick, & probably will not live much longer. It is his desire to see his children, Eliza, Anna & Mary, who are at your school, once more. He send the money to bring these children, if you will let them come, to remain for about two weeks.

When these children return to your Institute, their parents would like, also, to send a little boy, about nine years old, who seems to have quite a talent for drawing & molding. Please let them know, whether you have room for him, & whether you will take him at that time.

/s/ [Illegible signature]

The ledger provides us with specific information about the McCoonse children. Eliza McCoonse was nine when she arrived with the first group of Chippewa & Muncie children on September 16, 1884; Anna was seven when she arrived on December 6, 1884; and Mary was sent to Haskell at the age of six on October 1, 1887. About three weeks after the first McCoonse letter, the superintendent received another letter from Ottawa, Kansas.

Mar 11, 1888

Mr. Robinson

I wish you to tell the my daughters Eliza Annie & Mary & my little boy Albert, that their father died 8th of this month, rest of us are well and I want you to look after the children I don't want them to get lousy, when Annie came home this last time her head was sore and lousy and full of knits, she just got well when she return to Haskell I'll try to go and see them some time after payment in April please let us know How the children are getting along.

That is all for the present time

Yours Truly   Ellen McCoonse

Based on the records, it would appear that the children were not allowed to fulfill their father's last wish. According to the 1884–1889 ledger, Anna and Eliza were sent home on a furlough on June 20, 1888, after their initial four-year term was up, and they returned to Haskell on August 9, 1888. There are no additional remarks in Mary's ledger entry. This would lead one to conclude that the girls did not get to see their father prior to his passing.[37]

Interestingly, although the record indicates that none of the children was allowed to go home before their father passed away, their mother's letter seems to indicate otherwise. Her references "when Annie came home this last time" and "she just got well when she return to Haskell" imply that Annie was allowed to go home at least once after her arrival at Haskell. This contradicts the absence of information in Annie's ledger entry.

Additionally, there is the issue of the "little boy," Albert. Obviously he was in Ottawa, Kansas, with his parents when the first letter was written; yet he was at Haskell when the second letter was drafted roughly three weeks later. The ledger has Albert McCoonse, age nine, listed as arriving on March 1, 1888. Perhaps the two older girls were allowed to go home for a brief visit; when they were brought back to Haskell, their little brother came with them. It appears that the visit may have been unofficially authorized and so was not recorded. Perhaps the trade offered—a little boy for a dying request—was enough enticement to allow an unofficial bending of the rules. This is one little story about one sibling group; there are also other stories about other sibling groups at 19th century Haskell, what follows are some of those stories.[38]

Sibling Groups, Part I

Various sibling groups were at Haskell in its earliest years. Utilizing available records, I can almost piece together a hazy picture of the lives of some of these groups at Haskell. Their stories illustrate a wide range of experiences.

Tragic is a mere word, compared to the reality faced by some students. As various authors have pointed out, boarding school life was riddled with hardships ranging from malnutrition, overcrowding, death and disease to military rule and institutional labor, not to mention the blatant attack on Native identity. As shown in the most recently published theses and dissertations, students at Haskell certainly suffered the same traumas. Although these authors present an overview of some of the situations faced at Haskell, there are deeper stories of tragedy to be told.[39]

May Mahojah, full-blood Kaw, was seven when she arrived at Haskell on July 1, 1887, with her sister Ada Mahojah, who was ten. May did not make it through the winter; she passed away on December 18, 1887, and was buried in the Haskell cemetery. The lack of information in Ada's entry in the student ledger indicates that Ada remained at Haskell at least through 1889 without going home. Ada passed away in 1893 at the age of fifteen and was also buried in the school cemetery. The sisters arrived together at Haskell and now remain together in the Haskell cemetery. Interestingly, May's death is noted in the 1884–1889 handwritten student registration ledger, but her "official" student file in the National Archives does not list a date in the departure portion. Instead it states, "Dropped ?????" Logically, it would seem that her death was not listed in her "official" student file in order to minimize the number of deaths. Ada's student file, on the other hand, notes: "Dropped Jan. 21, 1893 (Death)." [40]

Based on this incident, as well as other information, it seems that the official student files may have been created in the summer of 1889, and deaths prior to that date were not necessarily recorded in the students' official school files. One can almost comprehend the motives of administration; at the same time, it raises the issue of forgotten children. In other words, as I look at May Mahojah's student file, it appears that she just disappeared. She was "Dropped???"; however, an obscure record and a tombstone tell a different story. Essentially, May became a forgotten child—perhaps to all but her sister Ada, until she too passed away. Their story is but one of the many waiting to be told.

Willie Sears, a fifteen-year-old Sioux, arrived at Haskell with his ten-year-old brother, Vincent, on September 15, 1887 from Kaw Agency, Indian Territory. In the 1884–1889 registration record, it is noted that Willie died on May 18, 1888. The cause of death listed in the ledger is "Accidentally killed." The meaning of that phrase, like so many other things about this early period, will remain forever a mystery. But this little story does not end there. The day after Willie was accidentally killed, in a letter dated May 19, 1888, Edgar McCassey wrote to the Superintendent:

> Hon. Gov. Robinson, Dear Sir:
> Both Willie and his brother were put in my charge and care last Sept. on leaving home. I promised to do all I can for Willie and Vincent but now that Willie is dead I feel it my duty to take the remains to his parents. By you sending them the remains they will know that you doing just what is best for both parents and children intrusted [sic] to your care.
> Mr. Sears has been in bed sick with Rheumatism for nearly two years and I hardly believe Mrs. Sears would come to see Willie. And another thing probably they will not hear of the death of Willie for a week or two for they live several miles below our Agency and sends once a month or so for provisions to the city. Mr. Sears is respected as a gentleman by every body that knew him and well off in life and this news will be quite a blow to them. I would rather, with your consent, take the remains at once to them for a letter will not reach them for five or sick [sic] day. Hoping for an early reply
> I close—Very Respectfully
> Edgar McCassey

Further investigation indicates that Edgar McCassey was a nineteen-year-old, full-blood Kaw student who also arrived on September 15, 1887, from the Kaw Agency. Although the actual connection between the Sears brothers and Edgar is unclear, the latter apparently felt an obligation to take Willie's remains home. Tragically, a headstone in the Haskell cemetery proves that Willie Sears never made it home to his parents. Edgar's request apparently was denied. In the end, Edgar McCassey "deserted July 11, 1889" and was "expelled" on July 13, 1889.[41]

These short stories of the Mahojah and Sears siblings illustrate the ultimate sacrifice paid by just three of the 19th century Haskell students. Although we don't know the actual circumstances surrounding any of the deaths, historical inquiry has allowed for some small part of their stories to be told. There are certainly other similar stories buried in the documents, but those stories will have to wait for another time. For now, I would like to redirect the discussion to other aspects of 19th century boarding school life, industrial training and the military atmosphere.

Industrial Training

As with other aspects of Haskell history, Anderson (1997) and Vuckovic (2001) have done an admirable job of detailing the industrial training aspects of the institution; therefore, this study does not expand in that area outside of providing the basic information.

When it opened, Haskell was advertised as a specialized vocational school with a major emphasis on agriculture. The literary component provided instruction in first, the English language, then progressing into subject matter from the first through fifth grades of the public schools. Although there certainly was an academic component that expanded within a decade after its founding, the students of 19th century Haskell still spent the majority of their time laboring to keep the school operational. According to Anderson (1996),

> Haskell had long practiced self-sufficiency, with Indian children producing the bulk of necessary food, clothing and shelter . . . student labor defrayed operational costs because the inmates were responsible for upkeep of the campus and eliminated a need to hire outside employees for most of the duties associated with running Haskell. Certainly the work of various industrial departments often consisted of maintaining and improving the physical condition of the school.[42]

Haskell's superintendent, during the second year of Haskell's existence, wrote in his 1886 annual report,

> The duties of each pupil comprise 4 hours of work on an industrial detail, 2 hours of study and recitation in the school room, 1 hour of evening study, with an omission of school-room work and evening study hour on Saturdays. A reduction of school-room work to 1½ hours daily is made during the summer, and during the hot weather there is an entire suspension of school work for those on the farm, garden, and several other details."

This type of schedule was fairly standard at Haskell, as well as at other boarding schools during the late 1800s.[43]

The following year, in 1887, Haskell Superintendent Charles Robinson, reported: "Pupils in attendance January 1, 1887, numbered 250, from 27 tribes." Also included in his annual report was a series of detailed tables listing the efforts of Haskell students. The information is reproduced in Table 2 in order to give some sense of the enormous amount of work that was required of the 19th century Haskell students. With the exception of the Carpenter's and the Wagon-maker's Departments, the lists have been reproduced in their entirety. The Carpenter's Department table also included a column for "Value of time" and "Total value," which contained dollar amounts for each item; these columns have been omitted, but the absolute totals have been included. As for the Wagon-maker's Department, the columns "Value" and "Value labor on wood" and their corresponding totals have not been included. All in all, the table illustrates an immense amount of work for just 250 students. Perhaps this is one of the reasons students deserted.[44]

Over time, there would be shifts in the labor force and duties of various groups of students at Haskell. For example, when the higher levels of education were introduced in 1894—preparatory, normal and commercial—the students in these departments were exempted from industrial training. Ultimately, however, Haskell continued to depend largely on student labor for the school's operation and maintenance for many decades.

Table 2: Student Production, 1887

The following are some of the productions and articles made or repaired from January 1 up to and including June 30, 1887:

Products of the farm

Articles	Quantity	Articles	Quantity
Wheat . . . . .bushels	156	Peas . . . . bushels	12
Corn (estimated) . . . . .do	300	Radishes . . . . .do	10
Oats . . . . do	1,100	Currants . . . . .do	10
Squashes . . . . .do	25	Parsnips . . . . .do	10
Potatoes . . . . .do	1,000	Tomatoes . . . . .do	50
Turnips . . . . do	5	Cucumbers . . . . do	2½
Beans . . . . do	20	Eggs . . . . dozen	51¼
Fruit, various . . . . do	1,000	Milk . . . . gallons	1,130
Onions . . . . do	10	Hay . . . . tons	75
Beets . . . . do	30	Butter . . . . .pounds	221

Mending department
Total number of garments repaired from February 11, date on which the mending room was made a regular feature of the industrial work, up to and including June 30, 1887, 4,521.

Tailoring department
Uniform coats made 128
Uniform pants made 33
Towels made 25
Pants (children's) made 13
Hickory Shirts made 108
Waists (children's) made 20

Shoemaking department
Pairs shoes made from
     April 20 to June 30, 1887. 146
Pieces harness repaired from
     April 20 to June 30, 1887 20

Table 2: Student Production, 1887 (Continued)

Sewing department

Articles	Number	Articles	Number
Wheat .... bushels	156	Peas .... bushels	12
Aprons	197	Bed-spreads	49
Clothes bags	30	Towels	87
Caps (knit)	7	Table-spreads	56
Desk covers	5	Towels (roller)	52
Ruffles	40	Handkerchiefs	48
Gowns (night)	6	Dresses (skirts ruffled)	113

Carpenter's department

Articles manufactured, repairs, etc. / Number

Ladder 14 feet long	1	Ladder 20 feet long	1
Revolving desks	2	Provision bins	2
Cupboard	2	Ice house	1
Carpenter's tool-chest	1	Carpenter's trestles	4
Book-case	2	Easel	1
Table 30 by 60 inches	1	Trestles building	3
Grain-bin	1	Meat-safe	1
Window-screens	99	Door	1
Wooden guns	200		

Work on shop building; Labor in repairs on hospital; Repairs on boys' building; Repairs on girls' building, Misc. repairs

Total "Value of time"	$ 768.7	Total "Total value"	$1,772.50

Wagon-maker's department

Articles manufactured

New work-bench; Cam-marker; Wagon doubletrees, at 75 cents (2); Plow doubletrees; Shafts in truck wagon (2); Shaft in cultivator; Thimble skein; Bottom in wagon-bed; Felloes in wagon-wheel (2) and New farm-wagon

Repairs, etc.

Dump-cart; haul-cart; lumber-wagon; truck; work-bench; spring wagon; wheelbarrow; cultivator; hay-rake; stone-barrow; Stone-boat; Sundries

---

Source: 1887 *Annual Report to the Commissioner of Indian Affairs*, 241–242.

Military Atmosphere

With the arrival of the second superintendent in September of 1885 came strict military discipline. All students of all ages, male and female, learned military drilling. Waking at 5:30 a.m. to the sound of bugles blaring reveille, the students marched everywhere—to meals, to work and to school. Their day ended as it began, with the sound of blaring bugles playing taps. With the introduction of the military discipline came the guard house. The guard house would be replaced by a jail built in 1910. The jail would remain on the campus and in use until 1932. Like the industrial training, the military discipline would also be a mainstay at Haskell for decades to come.[45]

One aspect of the military discipline that garnered attention from the local community was the marching of the students. In September 1900, *The Indian Leader* reprinted a comment from the local newspaper:

> One of the prettiest sights to be seen in the vicinity of Lawrence is that of the Indian school pupils as they march in to supper each evening at 5:30 o'clock. The boys and girls are formed in companies, and in command of company officers are marched toward the dining hall, and in the form of a hollow square are halted, and battalion officers take command. The band is stationed at the entrance to the dining hall, and as the officer gives the command "uncover," every boy doffs his hat and all stand at attention while a bugle call is sounded and the band plays "The Star Spangled Banner." Then the band plays a march and the pupils march to their supper. The work is done with a soldierly like precision that is very attractive, and the inspiring music of the band is certainly inclined to instill a feeling of patriotism in the hearts of the pupils. Many spectators, people who have rigs and can go to the school, are present at the exercises in the evening, and are amply repaid by the sight that greets them.—*Lawrence Journal.*[46]

It is important to note that although the military discipline may have been difficult for most students, many of the young men would make use of their military training when they later joined the armed forces to fight under the United States flag. A 1918 issue of *The Indian Leader* references a number of young Haskell men who joined the Army. The writer, updating his audience on his interactions with other Haskell alumni, writes, "Have seen Mr. Venne, Bill Williams, M. Kelly, L. Zane, and P. Willis. The boys are all well and all sergeants. They are mighty glad they got that 'fool' drilling, as some of them called it, at H.I. (Haskell Institute)."[47]

Conclusion: Sacrifice

The preceding accounts are intended to illustrate some of the examples of sacrifices made by 19th century Haskell students. It has not been an easy task to interpret the stories of sacrifice of these students. But without the help of a number of partial historical records, it would have been impossible. In the end, it is quite remarkable that this many stories could be gleaned from the meager sources. Some of the stories are no more than a name and an age; some illustrate solid connections between students, as well as between students and teachers. They are all valuable for what they tell us about early Haskell, as well as for the clues they provide about student life there in the 19th century. In the end it is my hope that I have portrayed some small measure of the sacrifices made in an earlier time.

This grainy photo (1884) shows the first three buildings: a boy's dorm, schoolhouse, and girl's dorm. It is likely that this is what the first students saw when they arrived at Haskell.

Photos courtesy of Haskell Cultural Center & Museum

With the labor of the male students, the institution quickly grew (1899).

After arriving at the institution the students, male and female, were introduced to military procedures through the cadet battalions.

At least four hours each day were spent engaged in industrial labor. For the male students, this included engineering (above, ca. 1900), b

For the female students, industrial labor meant kitchen detail, sewing and laundry.

(top photo, ca. 1886; bottom photo, ca. 1889)

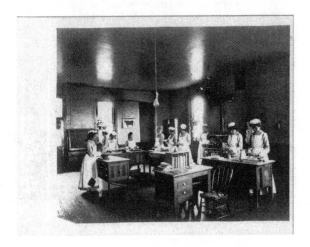

Cramped living quarters helped spread sickness. Meanwhile, three to four hours a day were spent in the classroom on a rotating schedule. Some students learned in the morning and worked in the afternoon, while others worked in the morning and spent the afternoon in the classroom.

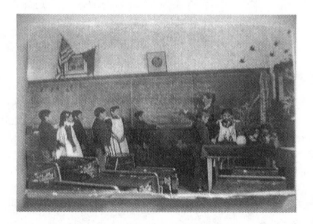

Charles Campbell letter, page one
Charles and Sara T.D. Robinson Collection, 1834-1911, Kansas State Historical Society

a you. Please tell me
how are you getting
along this spring.
I should like to know
very much if you
write to me. I glad. I
like to go home this
summer because I can
stay here this school
because I got sore my
neck this spring. I
want ask you some
money Please you sent
to me money and some
moccasins because
I like some money and
some moccasins too.
I tell you about my
Lesson third reader and
Geography and Arith-
etic, and Language
and Spelling, and all

Charles Campbell letter, page two

my Lesson of different words. and I trying hard to learn all Every thing. this month. well I guess stop writing letter for this time because I have nothing to say I think that is all

from your son

Charles E Campbell

answer very soon if you Please

Cheyenne & Arapahoe Agency

Washington Indian Territory

Charles Campbell letter, page three

PART III: STORIES OF STUDENT SURVIVAL

Although the earliest years at Haskell are filled with many examples of suffering and sacrifice, there are also stories of students who found ways to adapt to the difficult living conditions and to cope with the trauma that was all around them—they found ways to survive and prosper. Survival, in its simplest form, means doing what it takes to stay alive. In the stories that follow, the students did what they had to do. In many cases, survival included the act of embracing "white" education and all it had to offer.

In the boarding school literature, there are a variety of terms that become intertwined with the boarding school story, words such as assimilation, accommodation and resistance. All of these aspects can be found in the text that follows, and there are those who will see only acts of assimilation or accommodation. For example, readers might view some of the orations that were delivered by the students as extremely assimilationist in their titles and content matter. Certainly, all of the students were forced to assimilate to some degree, and there can be no doubt that many of them would absorb the entire concept, ultimately becoming "white" in thoughts, beliefs and mannerisms. However, there were also those who played the game of education without losing their birthright, their Nativeness.

One individual's story scattered within an earlier thesis on Haskell is that of Frank Eagle. I first encountered the name during a discussion of students who stayed at Haskell beyond the required initial term. The historian Anderson writes, "Frank Eagle, son of the Ponca chief White Eagle, came to Haskell after three years at Carlisle. He remained at Haskell almost ten years, from August 30, 1884, until February 16, 1894; he was eighteen when he arrived." The name appears again when Anderson writes, "During the summer vacation of 1887, Frank Eagle convinced several others to return to the school with him and wrote Robinson '18 children want to come [and] we will start any time if you send the tickets from Ponca to Lawrence.'" Anderson makes one final reference: "Frank Eagle, the Ponca chief's son who liked Haskell well enough to stay there for a decade, became the first president of Oklahoma's Native American Church in 1918 as the peyote cult reawakened the search for an Indian identity akin to the Ghost Dance rituals of thirty years earlier." These three, largely disconnected pieces of information tell a story about one student. It is the story of a student who came to the Haskell in the beginning and embraced the institution. But, in the end, he returned to his traditional heritage, a point Anderson makes in his final assessment that assimilation did not succeed at Haskell as it was planned. During my own research, I found a few more pieces of Frank Eagle's story. In the end, Frank Eagle's story illustrates the fact that students were often able to adapt to their institutional environment and espouse its virtues, and yet return to their Native ways at later times in their lives. In other words, they found ways to survive.[48]

What follows are wonderful stories of student survival. They illustrate students who embraced various survival mechanisms, many of which can be considered comparable to the student life found in mainstream higher education institutions of the time. The stories speak of students who not only embraced student life, but who sought to excel in it. In other words, they utilized aspects of the institution to grow and realize their potential. Some of the stories in this chapter were less difficult to construct than those in the last chapter, primarily because of the information that can be found in *The Indian Leader.*

Although many of the earliest issues of the Haskell campus newspaper, established in 1897, are overburdened with Christian values, patriotism and work ethic as attributes that are repetitiously present in the stories, there are brief references, sometimes only one sentence long, that provide information on former and current students. Additionally, the larger articles on programs and progress at the institution allow us limited access, but access nonetheless, to student life at Haskell. Ultimately, the newspaper has allowed me to gather more information to use in interpreting and constructing this story of stories.

In the following text, I present a varied collection of stories of individuals who embraced aspects of the student life on campus as a method of survival. Student life in this particular study focuses, largely, on the literary societies within the institution. Like the literary societies that emerged in the 1830s among the free "Negroes" and discussed by Porter (1936), the societies at Haskell had a large measure of value for the students who engaged in them by providing an avenue for intellectual growth, a platform for knowledge sharing, as well as encouraging, character-building and democracy. And like those found in the black colleges in the late 1800s and early 1900s, the literary societies at Haskell provided one of the "only real recreational and intellectual outlet[s]" for Native students who had little freedom and very few choices in any area of their daily lives. In the stories that unfold, it is obvious that most of the early Haskell students who were directly connected to the literary societies recognized the value of the societies and acted accordingly.[49]

It is important to note here that the actual literary societies at Haskell were restricted to the students in the upper levels of the educational realm, including the preparatory class, but especially those in the normal and commercial departments. Therefore, I do focus more on these areas of the educational arena in my text, devoting a larger amount of time to the normal department for reasons discussed later. In any case, although it appears that most of the students were not actually directly engaged with the societies, it seems that most were, at the very least, exposed to them in some manner. The activities of the societies, including orations, essays, dramas and music, found their way into all areas of Haskell in varied degrees. With that, I would like to begin with the ultimate story of survival and the most complete account of any one student's life that emerged from my research, the story of Elijah Brown.

Elijah Brown

Elijah Brown was twenty-four when he arrived at Haskell on November 3, 1897, to attend the Normal School, according to his student file. He was a member of the Mission Tribe from Cascade Locks, Oregon. It was probably one of the first days in July, 1898, when the superintendent received the following letter:

June 30, 1898

H.B. Peairs, Superintendent
  U.S. Indian Industrial School,
    Lawrence, Kansas.
Sir:
  You are hereby advised that authority has been granted for you to expend a sum not exceeding $75.00 (after July 1, 1898) in the open market purchase, delivered at the school, of an artificial limb for Elijah Brown, an Indian pupil attending said school, as per the quotation of Mr. B.F. Rounds, of Kansas City, Mo., as requested and for the reasons stated in your letters dated May 19 and June 14, 1898.
    Very Respectfully,
    /s/ A.G. Tonner, Acting Commissioner

Sometime prior to May, 1898, Elijah lost his leg while at Haskell. Interestingly, there is no reference to this issue in Elijah's student file. There is no indication of how the loss occurred; however, it is possible that Elijah may have had an on-the-job accident. He worked in the printing department as a member of *The Indian Leader* team from December, 1897, until he left Haskell in November, 1899.[50]

Although it is unclear how he lost his leg, what is clear is that Elijah continued at Haskell as a student for a period of time following the loss of his limb. In fact, it appears that Elijah was quite active; he played the roles of artist, orator and nurse during his time at Haskell.

His artwork was discussed in *The Indian Leader* on various occasions; the first reference is made in the March 1898 issue:

Our Reception
On February 23 Mrs. Doerfus gave a party for the little people, the boys and girls who are too small to go to study hour and other evening gatherings. A nice program consisting of recitations, dialogues and songs, was given by the wee ones. Miss Robbins sang, Jessie Swett played, the band gave several selections, Elijah Brown made some clever pictures, and then

came supper which was very nice and greatly enjoyed by the small guests. Some of the youthful gentlemen were very polite and gave their oranges and some of the other good things to the little girls. The grand march was the next thing. In this both large and small took part. Just before ten o'clock the little ones, tired, sleepy, but very happy, said good night to their kind hostess and were soon dreaming of "our reception."[51]

Not only does the information on the event provide us with knowledge about Elijah, but it also gives us some indication of the student life at 19th century Haskell. Six months later, in October, 1898, Elijah's artwork was displayed at a local fair. A group of students went to the fair "in Bismarck Grove, such a beautiful place, about five miles from here [where] Elijah Brown has some clever pencil drawings on exhibition."[52]

As an orator, Elijah kept himself busy. The first mention of his talent is found in the April, 1898, issue; he was one of three students who gave a recitation at a program held on April 22. Three months later, on June 20, 1898, Elijah was involved in the commencement exercises. It was noted in *The Indian Leader*:

> Christopher Cournoyer in an address to the lower classes bequeathed to them many things to have and to hold and gave them sound advice about improving their minds that they might in some slight measure fill the places left vacant by the class of '98. Elijah Brown made the response for the lower classes very cleverly.

As will be noted in a later section, this type of exchange was common in student life in mainstream institutions. It provides an example of the similarities between Haskell student life and college and secondary student life as it existed at the time.[53]

The following fall, in October, 1898, Elijah was promoted to the Junior Normal class and joined The Athenian Society, one of the two male literary societies at Haskell that year. In March of 1899, Elijah entered the oratorical contest held at Haskell:

The long talked of contest among representatives of the normal, commercial and training classes took place last Monday
evening . . . The first speaker was Elijah Brown of the normal
class. The subject of his oration was 'Why are We Here?' His
voice was clear and enunciation excellent."[54]

Elijah Brown's oration was printed in an April 1899 issue of *The Indian
Leader*. A lengthy text, it is presented here in its entirety:

Why Are We Here?
We are here to solve the Indian problem. We are here to shat-
ter the theory that the only good Indian is a dead one and to
convince the world that an American Indian has a mind to
cultivate and a soul to be saved. We are here to verify the statement that the Indian is capable of reaching the highest plane
of intellectual, physical and moral development. We are here
to aid our people by fitting ourselves to be their servants, and
to aid ourselves by learning the great secret of a successful life.
We are here because we live under a Christian government
which has seen fit to establish schools for our use that we may
become an intelligent part of this great nation.

It is well that as time passes and we advance step by step, that
we stop and ask ourselves the all important question "why are
we here?" We are likely to forget and drift along with the tide
of events instead of breasting the waves in the struggle for the
prize we are here to obtain. Homer, in relating the wander-
ings of Ulysses, the hero of Troy, describes a beautiful island
inhabited by the Lotus Eaters. Here the sorrows and pains of
the world were unknown, and as soon as the stranger partook
of the mysterious flower, he forgot home and friends, and for
the remainder of his life was content to bathe in luxury and
enjoyment.

Here, we have everything needful for the care of the body
and the cultivation of the mind, without money and without
price. We enjoy privileges that are enjoyed by no other people.

Are not we prone to forget and become as the Lotus Eaters of that enchanted spot and to become dead to the world until we are suddenly confronted with the great problems of life? Let us again ask ourselves "why are we here?" and if we have forgotten the object of our mission, let us muster our forces and concentrate them upon a purpose, and hold them there until that purpose is accomplished.

This world is a great field of action. Life is a struggle for an existence and the weak must fall, while the strong conquer. It is true that the white man is several hundred years in advance, but that should not discourage us in our efforts to succeed in life. It is only through difficulties that mankind rises to a higher plane in civilization. The Gods have placed sweat in the pathway of excellence. Look upon the colored man for an example. Only thirty years ago, the shackles of slavery fell from his limbs. Today we behold him in the marts of trade, amid the branches of learning and a laborer in every profession. Are we not able to rise to the same heights? Can not we accomplish great things? We can, for whatever man has done man can do. We are soon to join the ranks of those who are wrestling a subsistence from the world and it is to fit ourselves for that ordeal that we are here. As education has become a necessary part of a young man's equipment and if he possess it not he is forced out from the front rank as being unqualified, and must follow in the rear, a burden to himself and an impediment to progress.

We are not to confine our entire time and expend our every energy in getting and storing up gold and silver. We are a part of society and are to come into contact with men and women. We are so constituted that we cannot live by ourselves and for ourselves but must share our joys and our sorrows with our fellow men. Then we are here to be educated in the ways of society, so that we shall be enabled to intermingle with social organizations. If we are not enlightened on this important subject, we shall forever be debarred from the pleasure of the best human fellowship. The humblest citizen can aspire to reach the highest position of honor in the nation.

We live in a free government where all men are equal. Self-government is the greatest blessing the American citizen enjoys. There comes a time in the life of every young man when he must cross his Rubicon and cast his lot with a political party. It is an important step in life, and should be considered well before it is taken. Each of us must take the step. How shall it be taken? Shall we follow the custom of the great majority by being what our fathers have been? No! let us study for ourselves and choose our own platforms and stand thereon till events show whether we are right or wrong. Let us not listen to the voice of the many sided demagogue until we are persuaded to do his bidding, but let us be self-made citizens. We are here to fit ourselves for citizenship, so that when we enter the arena of action, we shall be able to know the right from wrong and the true from the false. Our knowledge of this great subject will enable us to represent our people well, and to shield them from the injustice that has for so many years been their sad lot.

The highest life a man can live is a Christian life. There is nothing higher to which mankind can aspire than to imitate the "Man of Sorrows" who went about comforting the broken hearted, giving sight to the blind and strength to the lame.

It is to acquire this pearl of great price that we are here. Let us lay hold of it and clasp it to our hearts, for it is the most precious gem ever possessed by man. With its radiance as a flashlight, we shall never drift out as wrecks upon the sea of life. We shall weather every storm and at last complete a successful journey and enter the haven of peace.

I expect to pass through this life but once. If, therefore, there is any kindness I can show or any good I can do to any fellow being let me do it now. Let me not deter or neglect it, for I shall not pass this way again.[55]

Elijah was awarded first place in the contest. And although it is lengthy, I present it in its entirety because this essay tells us much about the education at 19th century Haskell. First, it illustrates that "The Indian Problem" was familiar to the students, as well as giving us some indication of what that phrase meant to students. It also gives us some sense of the depth of the history and Christian principles that Elijah was taught. Finally, it is an example of how some Native students perceived their education. Elijah saw education as a way to rise above the place where his father stood. That summer, the summer of 1899, Elijah attended the Normal Institute in Lawrence. Apparently this was a local summer school for emerging teachers. In the fall of 1899, he returned to Haskell and was elected the president of The Athenian Society, one of the existing literary societies.[56]

Elijah's nursing aptitude emerged as he worked to care for a sick friend, evidenced by an entry in the May 15, 1899, *Indian Leader* issue: "Elijah Brown developed into a very efficient nurse during the illness of Nelson Swamp." Nelson Swamp's obituary gives some insight into the reality of the times. It states in part:

> Although not unexpected the death of little Nelson Swamp on the morning of May 6 was a shock to many. Nelson was not a strong child as he has suffered for years with some nervous trouble. When the pupils were having the measles a few weeks ago Nelson contracted the disease. Pneumonia followed and in his weak condition he could not rally from it.

Nelson Swamp, Oneida, was nine years old when he arrived at Haskell on September 26, 1896, from Oneida, Wisconsin. At this point, little else is known about Nelson Swamp outside of the fact that Elijah Brown cared for him prior to his death.

In October of the same year, Elijah, along with another Haskell student, served as nurse again when another friend fell ill. The entry in *The Indian Leader* states: "Peter Herron and Elijah Brown assisted in caring for Frank Shaw during the latter part of his illness." Frank Shaw, a formerly active Haskell student who had moved into Lawrence and married earlier that summer after finishing his education, died of consumption on October 17, 1899.

One month after Frank Shaw's death, Elijah was called to his nursing position again, only this time, it was not for one of his fellow students. It was for his father: "Elijah Brown started for San Francisco last Wednesday morning. He was called there by the illness of his father. Elijah expects to go to work when he reaches his destination. We hope he will be successful; also that his father may recover."[57]

One further aspect of Elijah Brown emerges by the inclusion of his name on the Haskell Institute employee listing filed with the 1898 Annual Report to the Commissioner of Indian Affairs. Elijah, along with Homer Lewis, Robert Keith and Andrew Jackson (this is probably the "second" Andrew Jackson), is listed as a sergeant at a salary of $60; his date of appointment was January 1, 1898. It is unknown if or for how long Elijah actually served in this position. The positions on the list were naturally scheduled to conclude with the end of the fiscal year, dependent upon renewal for the following year. The 1899 employee listing does not list the position of sergeant; the position was probably made into one without compensation.

At this point, there is no clear definition for "sergeant" in this context, but there are clues. First, it was likely connected with the military system initiated by Superintendent Grabowski in 1885. In his annual report he wrote: "A cadet battalion organization of five companies broke up the tribal associations ... A better supervision of the pupils in dormitories, on playgrounds, &c., was also secured through the agency of the cadet officers attached to such an organization." Surely there was a rank designated "sergeant" that would have been considered an officer's position. The position of sergeant only appears on the 1898 employee list (but the 1892 list does include two positions for an "Officer of the day"). Making inferences, I have concluded that Elijah was a sergeant in one of the cadet battalions who was paid for a short time to help maintain order on the campus. In the end, although Elijah's terms of employment are unknown, the fact that he was a sergeant, even if for a short time, reflects leadership in his character.[58]

Although Elijah's official student file does not reflect his injury nor his accomplishments, it does contain information regarding his academic record and his departure:

June 20, 1899 Passed to Sr., Normal, must make up algebra
Nov. 14, 1899 Withdrawn—last few months of school work good
    Goes to San Francisco, California to seek work and to care for his father
Oct. 1, 1901 Dropped ("previous to date" handwritten on record)

It is unclear why Elijah is listed as "withdrawn" in 1899, yet not "dropped" until almost two years later. One thing is certain, however; Elijah eventually returned to his home state and secured a job with another off-reservation boarding school, one that he was familiar with. Elijah had attended Chemawa—established in Chemawa, Oregon, in February 1880—prior to his arrival at Haskell. Upon his return to his alma mater, Elijah utilized skills he had apparently acquired at Haskell, as he became the editor of Chemawa's newspaper.[59]

Elijah's obituary is printed in a September 1901 issue of *The Indian Leader*.

Elijah Brown

From the Chemawa American the following tribute to Elijah Brown, a graduate of the Haskell Normal department is copied: We are pained to announce the sudden death of E. Brown, editor of the Chemawa American, which occurred on August 28th, after a short illness. Elijah, as he was generally known, was a student of Chemawa for several years. Later on he attended Carlisle school and the Haskell Institute returning to Chemawa to assume charge of The American. He was a good faithful pupil and a bright, original, young man. His ability as a public speaker and a debater is well known wherever he has been.

While at Haskell he captured the first prize at the oratorical contest at the school.

As an editor and newspaper man he has been very successful.

Chemawa will miss Elijah in many ways. The American will also miss his energetic hand and inventive, humorous mind, as many of his articles showed considerable talent as a writer and were seasoned with a great deal of wholesome humor.

Elijah was president of the Chemawa Y.M.C.A. and has been a delegate to the Y.M.C.A. convention for many years. He was a member of the Methodist church and a good active Christian worker. We mourn the loss of a faithful pupil and an exemplary employee.[60]

As can be seen from his obituary, Elijah appears to have made the most of his education in the short time he had to live. He espoused the Christian virtues he had no doubt learned in the government Indian schools, he exhibited a solid character, and he illustrated good work ethic. At this point, it is obvious that Elijah Brown was a prime example of the success of the Indian education through assimilation model. His story could end here and I could be satisfied that the depth of his character has been discovered. But perhaps there was even more depth to Elijah Brown, abilities and knowledge that did not get measured or recorded in his student file, but that lie buried in a newspaper blurb and consequently allow us to enjoy one more tidbit of this wonderful young man's life.

In 1919, *The Indian Leader* printed an extensive alumni update that worked to share any available information about past graduates. Although Elijah does not have an entry—meaning he didn't actually graduate from Haskell—he is referred to in another former student's update.

John V. Plake had arrived as a young boy at Haskell during its first year and essentially grew up at the institution, ultimately graduating in 1897 from the commercial department. According to the alumni update:

> As a member of the original commercial class John studied politics as a side issue. It was during this time that William J. Bryan first came into the limelight with his 16-to-1 platform—free and unlimited coinage of silver. John began studying the issue of the day. He found in Elijah Brown another 16-to-1 man and they together were the Tammany Hall of Haskell. They could be seen on Saturday afternoons on the streets of Lawrence advocating their views to the farmers.[61]

This is interesting because it illustrates the fact that there was a certain amount of freedom afforded to the older male students in the last few years of the 19th century. Additionally, it is a display, not only of political awareness on the part of Native students, but also of the confidence of two young Native Haskell students in espousing their political views within the dominant society.

On the other hand, it also raises a question: How is it John and Elijah knew one another if the former graduated in June, 1897, according to *The Indian Leader*, yet the latter did not arrive until November, 1897, according to his student file? This serves as another solid example of some of the inconsistencies to be found in reviewing the early Haskell records. It seems that the student files are less reliable than some of the other information. In this case, there is certainly more information about the student printed in the newspaper than contained in his student file. It appears that Elijah's student file did not reflect the reality of his situation, so the information within is questionable. Of course, his is not the only such case.

As a final note on Elijah Brown, is it possible that this young man, about twenty-eight or twenty-nine when he passed away, died, in part, due to the very education he received at Haskell? In January, 1909, almost eight years after his death, *The Indian Leader* devoted five and a half-pages of a six-page paper to the reprinting of an article on tuberculosis. Originally published in the December *Southern Workman*,

"The International Congress of Tuberculosis," by J.E. Davis, detailed the Washington exhibit that culminated with The Sixth International Congress on Tuberculosis that was held from September 28-October 3, 1908. In one portion of the article, the author writes: "Printers are among the tradesmen most liable to tuberculosis."[62] I have not researched this subject, but I do have an opinion at this point. It is possible that this information was unknown a decade earlier. And one can assume that non-Native printers were just as susceptible as Native printers to the disease. Elijah worked with *The Indian Leader* throughout his time at Haskell, so he was trained in printing. In other words, did his job as a printer subject him to tuberculosis, of which he would die at a relatively early age? The connection between Elijah's education and his death is not an accusation it is just one example of students who took advantage of the education, persevered and seemingly succeeded in dominant society, only to become a victim of circumstances of the boarding school system.

Elijah's story is perhaps the most complete of the stories to be uncovered; it is a story of survival. Altogether, it gives us some indication of a thriving student life at 19th century Haskell. It illustrates some extent of the caliber of education that the Native students were receiving. It also provides clues and bits of information that help in constructing other stories.

Now that Elijah's story of survival has been told, it is time to share other stories of survival that are smaller, but valuable in their own right.

Building Communities

As stated earlier, the military system was introduced at Haskell by the second leader, Superintendent Grabowski, as a means to break up the tribal associations among students. However, he didn't anticipate that many of the students would adapt so quickly to their environment.[63]

Students, separated from their own communities and tribes, became connected with the students from other communities and tribes. Together, they built new communities that provided them with the emotional, physical and psychological support to help them survive the sometimes devastating conditions they lived under. Allegiances among the older students in military and social groups began to form. Students united and began to seek change. In fact, students were actively questioning the conditions of their environment as early as 1887.

In December of that year, a group of seven students submitted a petition to the Superintendent requesting an end to the early morning bugle call in the boys' dormitory. The petition reads as follows:

Hon. Charles Robinson

The undersigned being satisfied that blowing the bugle each morning as at present practiced in the different halls of the boys dormitory for the purpose of awakening the pupils is unnecessary.

Would respectfully respond that in addition to the two bells which are regularly sounded, there is generally noise enough in the above named dormitory from 5 until 6 a.m. to awaken the most proficient sluggard in all the land.

We would further state that no bugle was required to awaken the students last winter, or the past summer and we do not see the necessity of it now. That if pupils do not get up, the loss of several morning meals will in all probability touch their hearts in such a manner as to cause them to perform this duty.

Or if they must be awakened by other means than the regular belles (sic), we would suggest that it will not require any more time for the bugles to awaken the Captains of the ? companies, then he commences each morning in blowing upon the instrument (illegible).

While we may seem to be noting a rather insignificant matter and this petition may appear out of place to our contemplating the call to arms at a safe distance. Yet those who are compelled to listen to the disagreeable trumpeting at short range it is of some importance, and will all due respect the very one concerned your petitioners most respectfully request

that you have the nuisance abated.
Paul Hogan, James Spencer, Lidie Allen,
George R., L. May Kennedy,
Bertha Aspell & Lillie M. Hogan[64]

This petition illustrates that the students were obviously comfortable enough with the administration to take this action. Of course, it does leave one question: How and where did Native students get the idea to create a petition in the first place? One would assume that the thought came from one of the teachers at Haskell, but who and why? I can only guess.

Incidentally, the request was denied. In fact, reveille would continue to awaken Haskell students until the early 1930s. In spite of the rejection, students of that time would continue to utilize petitions to question administration, even to the point of subtly demanding accountability from those in charge of the institution.

Why Are We Dying?

In May of 1888, nineteen young men submitted a petition questioning the number of student deaths at Haskell. In the previous ten months, at least thirteen Haskell students had died. Jessie Murie, a 15-year-old Pawnee, succumbed to pneumonia on the same day the petition was submitted. The concise petition read as follows:

We, the undersigned pupils of Haskell desire to know what is the cause of so many deaths amongst us. There has been no such case known to us before. Surely there must be something wrong somewhere, either in the medicine or care that is taken of them.
/s/Edgar McCassey, Lamotte Primeaux, Frank Eagle, Dudley Shawnee, Sam Noble, Peter Bourassa, Thomas Kemmis, George Howell, Webb Hayes, Josiah Patterson, L.W. Miller, Edward Oger, Nicodemus Herr, Moore Van Horn, Kiser

Young Man, Lincoln Kennedy, William Pearce, Joseph Maigle, Reid Winney[65]

The young men who signed the petition, aged 16–27, came from ten different tribes. Some of them had been at Haskell since the beginning, some arriving only a year earlier. The nineteen spoke with a collective voice. Perhaps the collective voice of the students played a small part in the change in medical care. Superintendent Robinson had already replaced a nurse who was skimming rations; he replaced the physician within a month of the petition.

A brief glimpse at three of the young men who signed the petition illustrates the worst reality of the Haskell experience in the early years. One of the students, George Howell, a nineteen-year-old Pawnee, had arrived at Haskell with a group of nineteen Pawnee children on December 15, 1886. Also in the group was George's brother, Eberhald, who was fourteen years of age. Eberhald passed away on March 1, 1887, and was buried in the Haskell cemetery. Another Pawnee student, Webb Hayes, who had arrived with the same Pawnee group as George and who also signed the petition, contracted pneumonia and died on July 27, 1889. Perhaps George knew or was related to Jessie Murie and/or Webb Hayes (since all three were Pawnee); in any case, George is listed as "deserted" on October 28, 1889. A third student who signed the petition was also among those who would never leave Haskell. Josiah Patterson, introduced earlier, was also Pawnee; he passed away in 1893 at the age of 25. All four of these Pawnee men are buried in the Haskell Cemetery.[66]

In stark contrast, a glimpse of another student who signed the petition illustrates a different view of Haskell. Frank Eagle, a Ponca discussed earlier, was among the first group of students to arrive at Haskell on August 30, 1884. According to the Haskell 1884–1889 registration ledger, Frank departed in August of 1887 after his term expired. We know that he spent at least part of his first summer at home recruiting new students for Haskell; seemingly, he returned with eighteen pupils. Additionally, Frank Eagle is listed among the first graduates to finish the educational course in 1889, yet he continued at Haskell for an additional five years. An update included in the 1919 alumni special to *The Indian Leader* reads: "Frank Eagle is farming, has a good home, a wife, and five children. He was one of our fine singers when in school and, it is said, still sings a good deal. His address is Bliss, Okla."[67]

As discussed earlier, Anderson (1997) does provide additional information on Frank Eagle, notably that he was one of the boarding school graduates who "went on to become leaders in latter-day Pan-Indian movements."[68] This is clear evidence that although assimilation worked to some degree, sometimes in later years, students returned to their traditional grounding. In other words, assimilation had its limits. Furthermore, it is apparent (and has been stated by other authors) that government-run boarding schools actually helped to promote the Pan-Indian movement. But as that subject is not the issue of this narrative, I will return to the current subject matter by introducing one sibling group that embraced the survival tools of 19th century Haskell individually and collectively, the Plakes.

Sibling Groups, Part II

There is at least one sibling group who all survived the traumas of early Haskell and parlayed their education into successful dominant societal life skills. There were six Plake children, five boys and one girl; all six attended Haskell and at least five of them eventually graduated from the higher departments.

James was ten and John was seven when they arrived at Haskell on December 17, 1884, with a group of six other Chippewa and Muncie children from the nearby Ottawa reservation. This was the second group of Chippewa and Muncie youth to arrive at Haskell in its initial year; the first group of eight arrived on September 16, 1884, the day before Haskell's official opening ceremony. The only Plake girl, Nellie, was 8 years old when she joined her older brothers at Haskell on August 6, 1886.[69]

Prior to the summer of 1887, John & Josie Plake wrote a letter to Superintendent Charles Robinson requesting their children be allowed a visit home. The letter reads as follows:

Ottawa Kansas May 29th 1887
Supt Dear Sir
    Now I take the opportunity to write a few lines in regard for my children will you Please and tell me whether you will be willing to sent them home during vacation or through the hot whether we would like to have them home. Their will be no trouble in returning them back I think it will do them good to get home once in a year they would study better and refreshes them we are very anxious to have the come we got a letter from Jimmy our oldest boy he said he like the school and the supt is good to us, but we would like to be at home on a visit so we could see all the loved ones at home there are three James and Johnnie and Nellie Plake
This is our humble prayer
From John and Josie Plake[70]

It appears that the request was not granted, at least not until the following year. The records indicate that James, John and Nellie were allowed to go home on June 30, 1888. Nellie was allowed "home on a furlough" and returned in August 1888. Meanwhile, the "term expired" for her two older brothers; however, they both returned on September 7, 1888, to begin another term. In spite of the fact that they were apparently refused a visit from their three children during the summer of 1887, Mr. and Mrs. Plake sent a third son, William, to Haskell on September 1, 1887. For some unknown reason, "Willie" was sent home on furlough on April 8, 1888, but he returned to Haskell on September 2, 1888. All four of the siblings were then allowed to go home on sixty days furlough from June 30, 1889, to August 31, 1889. The Plake siblings continued on in their education and were later joined at Haskell by younger brothers, Charles and Arthur Clinton.[71]

    Of the six siblings, five ultimately graduated from the higher departments, Normal and Commercial, which were introduced in 1894 and 1895, respectively. James and John both graduated in 1897 from the Commercial Department; Nellie was an 1899 Normal graduate; William was a Commercial graduate in 1900; and Charles followed in the footsteps of his brothers when he graduated from the Commercial department in 1903.

Based on a 1919 alumni update printed in *The Indian Leader*, the older five siblings were all successful. All worked for the Indian Service at some point; James, the oldest, was still with the Indian Service at the time of the update. Three of the brothers moved onto other careers: John was a rancher in Colorado; and William and Charles were working for oil companies in Tulsa, Oklahoma. Nellie's update discussed various teaching positions over time, but failed to clarify her status.[72]

Unlike the other five, less is known about Arthur Clinton Plake's stay at Haskell. He did not have the opportunities presented to his siblings — as noted earlier, the Commissioner of Indian Affairs ordered both the Normal and Commercial Departments to close in the middle of the 1902 school year. Although the Commercial Department would reorganize in 1906, it would take years for the program to rebuild. Two years younger than Charles, Arthur may have determined that the higher-level programs would not reappear at Haskell and therefore moved on prior to their re-establishment. In any case, it would appear that Arthur might have pursued his education after leaving Haskell; like the other Plake children, he worked for the Indian Service at some point in his career.

The two oldest Plake brothers, James and John, were listed as "1/8" Chippewa and Muncie (or just Muncie) on the first registration record; there is no blood quantum listed for Nellie and William. Naturally, with so little Native blood, the Plake siblings looked white, as evidenced by various photographs. Therefore, is it fair to wonder how this fact affected their survival, considering the hardships of the earliest years? For example, I assume that they were subject to the same ailments as the general Haskell student population, yet all six, at least four of whom spent thirteen years at Haskell, survived the various bouts of sickness.

Consider John, who was seven years old and listed as "good" under the "Condition" column of the 1884–1889 Haskell student registration ledger when he arrived at Haskell. However, the 1919 alumni update states that "John was rather a frail youngster." If John was indeed "frail," how is it that he survived when others did not? That is an unanswerable question, of course, but worth consideration. Perhaps his immunity levels were higher to certain afflictions because of his familial exposure to non-Native blood and/or environment. A more disturbing thought is, perhaps because of his skin color, he had lighter work details, less exposure to danger and/or better access to food and medicine due to preferential treatment by institutional staff. This would certainly not be beyond the realm of possibility, considering the attitudes and perceptions about Native peoples during that time.

On a positive note, John Plake was just one of many Haskellites who would meet his future spouse at Haskell. Edna Nevitt was in the Normal class and graduated in 1899, the same time as Nellie Plake. After graduation, Edna taught in Utah, then: "After a year or two she married John Plake, the culmination of a romance which began at Haskell" and took up the role of a rancher's wife in Colorado. This is but one example of the hundreds of romances over time that would begin at Haskell.[73]

Altogether, the story of the Plakes illustrates a sibling group who survived some of the toughest years of institutional history and embraced the opportunity provided them at Haskell. In a very real sense, they learned their survival skills at Haskell, both literally and figuratively. They had to survive the earliest years, long before electricity, running water and the like came to campus; they had to survive the various bouts of sickness that swept across the campus, as well as the military discipline and labor. At the same time, they were preparing to survive in dominant society by making the most of their educational journey. They all participated in various extra-curricular activities, evidenced by the concrete examples of their participation in student life found scattered in the pages of *The Indian Leader*. In the end, there is no doubt in my mind that the ultimate success of the Plake children had much to do with their access to the student activities that were available at 19th century Haskell.

Student Activities

Although students continued to be governed by strict military sched-
ules through the end of one century and into the next, they were
encouraged to pursue extra-curricular activities. The evolution and
extent of student activities at Haskell during the 19th century is vague.
It is clear that during the 1891–92 school year, the options for students
included band, choir, glee club, debate and Y.M.C.A. By 1908, the list
had grown to include at least four literary societies, a home economics
club, a mandolin club and Y.W.C.A. Baseball, the first organized sport
at Haskell, arrived in 1890, and the team became renowned quickly.
Football followed and, like Carlisle's teams, also quickly gained legend-
ary status.

Basketball was introduced in earnest in January of 1900 and quickly
became a campus-wide sport, played by faculty and all levels of students. The first mention of basketball can be found in the second issue
of *The Indian Leader* of the new century: "Basket-ball is the favorite
amusement with some of the gentlemen just now."[74] It appears that
the first "official" game was played the following week:

> A very exciting game of basket ball was played last Saturday
> evening in the gymnasium by a Haskell team and the Junior
> team from the State University [KU]. The members of the
> Haskell team are Chauncey Archiquette, Edward Valley, Simon
> Payer, Herbert Fallis and Frank James. Dr. Naismith acted as
> referee and Mr. Plank, Thomas St. Germaine, Theodore Perry
> and the manager of the K.U. team were the umpires. The
> work of the Haskell boys was fine, but the K.U. players were
> more expert in putting the ball in the basket as they were us-
> ing their own ball, while the Haskell boys have been playing
> with a football. The result of the game was a tie.[75]

By March 1900, the basketball team was traveling to other gymnasi-
ums to play the new game:

Basket Ball with the Tigers

The Y.M.C.A. gymnasium at Kansas City was crowded last night with basket ball enthusiasts, gathered to witness the battle royal between the Y.M.C.A. Tigers and the Indians from Haskell Institute. When the game was ended the Indians had lost to the Tigers by a score of 31 to 11.

The Indians during the first half, put up a rattling good game, playing a fast, aggressive contest and displaying many original ideas, in their team work. But after their brilliant stand in the first part the Tigers went at them in such a terrible manner, and scored goals with such regularity, that the Kansans lost hope. During the first half Archiquette threw two of the most wonderful goals ever seen on a Kansas City basket ball field. He plays back, and standing under his opponent's basket and in less then three minutes, twice threw the ball the full length of the field and straight into the net. Both throws were little less than marvelous, and for days to come will remain the record of the Y.M.C.A. field.

The fast work of the Haskells at the start took the champions by surprise and it was not until the last part of the first half that they began displaying their usual team work. Besides Archiquette's two baskets, Payer made three free throws during the first twenty minutes of play. The Haskell boys deserve much praise for the good, clean, manly game they played. At no time during the contest did they resort to burly tactics, playing throughout a clean, gentlemanly game.

The Haskell players were Valley, forward; Fallis, forward; Payer, center; Archiquette, back; Johnson, forward.—*Kansas City Journal.*[76]

In the following week's issue of *The Indian Leader*, there are multiple references to the game, including a short paragraph about a home game with the Topeka Y.M.C.A. that ended with a score of "26–16 in favor of the visitors," as well as notification that "two regular basket ball teams have been organized among the employees." On the same page is the following entry:

Willie Jerome in a letter home thus describes basket ball: There is not much to think about in what extra time we have except basket ball. But as you probably do not know what basket-ball is I might as well explain it to you. It is a game in which a round foot-ball is used. Five players constitute a team. There are two goals. At each goal is an iron hoop, about ten feet from the floor and which should be parallel with the floor. The point in the game is to throw the ball into the hoops, which counts, if done in the field two and when done on account of a foul, one.[77]

The first basketball season was short, giving way to baseball in April; however, over time it is evident that the students embraced the game, becoming a formidable opponent for years to come. At the same time, April, 1900, saw the introduction of a new club:

The Athletic Club
There was organized last Friday, the Haskell Institute Athletic Club. The purposes of this organization are to foster and promote all forms of athletic sport and to exercise general control over the same.

At the head of the organization is the Athletic Board consisting of nine members, the superintendent, four employes [sic] appointed by him and four students elected by the student members of the association. The officers of the club are: President, Superintendent Peairs; vice-president, Chauncey Archiquette; secretary, Simon H. Payer; treasurer, J. W. Alder; general manager, U.S.G. Plank.

No change will be made at present in the management of the various teams already established, but it was voted to organize a track-athletic team and Omer Gravelle was chosen manager of the same. This system consolidates all athletic in-

terests, and will undoubtedly be instrumental in encouraging
a spirit of true sport among the students.[78]

Ultimately, it appears clear that from the beginning of their introduction, Haskell students didn't just pursue the various extra-curricular activities, they excelled.[79]

M. Vuckovic (2001) illustrates this point in her detailed discussions of music and athletics at Haskell in her book *Onward Ever, Backward Never: Student Life and Student Lives at Haskell*. She also spends time outlining the Young Men's Christian Association (Y.M.C.A.) in her discussion about the role of religion at Haskell. Therefore, I have chosen not to explore those areas in my text outside of general references. Instead, I will focus on the literary societies and other social activities, a discussion that is missing in the literature.

There is no clear reference to the actual beginning of literary societies at Haskell, but there was at least one in existence as early as 1889. There is no annual report from Haskell's Superintendent for that year; Oscar Leonard apparently did not file one. This is understandable considering Leonard only took the position under protest and with the promise that a replacement would be found as soon as possible. In the meantime, Daniel Dorchester, Superintendent of Indian Schools, included an update on Haskell in his annual report. About his visit to the institution in May, 1889, he wrote, "This school has a literary society in which debates are conducted. The Indian problem and other great questions are often discussed and 'settled,' and the speakers exhibit much genuine eloquence." There is no further mention of societies in the annual reports until 1894 when Superintendent Swett wrote, "Several well organized literary societies and Christian organizations did splendid work all through the year. The boys' debating club deserves especial mention for the excellent work done throughout the entire term."[80]

In Swett's 1895 annual report, he presented the information in a more detailed fashion, including more distinct categories that began with boldface type. Nestled between the "Classroom" and "Religious organizations" was the following entry:

> Literary societies.—The boys and girls have had separate organizations, and some very excellent work has been done. Especially is this true of the boys' debating club, which was maintained throughout the year and met once each week. Some question of interest was discussed at each meeting by members of the society, and each week one was appointed to discuss current topics. Thus all members of the society were kept well informed on the news of the times.
>
> Besides this work, some author's life and works were studied each month, so that at the end of the year the student had become acquainted with many of the thoughts of our best writers.[81] (p. 374)

This is the first mention of gender in the societies; it tells us that there were at least two societies, one for girls and one for boys. It is unclear if Swett's description of specific activities is in reference to the debating club or a literary society. Perhaps they were one and the same. It is also not clear if the girls' society engaged in the same activities.

In his 1896 annual report, Swett largely discards the titled sections. The running narrative following "Literary department" includes the following:

> More than usual interest has been shown in the work of the literary societies during the past year. Two societies, one for boys and one for girls, have been maintained, and many interesting and instructive programmes [sic] rendered. The greatest improvement in this work has been along the line of original composition and essay writing. An interesting and successful entertainment was an oratorical contest in which ten pupils of the advanced grades participated. Listeners to the orations pronounced them very thoughtful, and spoke of the contest as marking a new epoch in Indian education, because it demonstrated the ability of young Indian people to think for themselves.[82]

Based on this excerpt, it appears that the boys' debate society and literary society discussed in the previous annual report may have been one and the same. On another note, the structure of the sentence about the oratorical contest seems to indicate that this was a new aspect of the societies; it sounds like that was the first contest held at Haskell. Altogether, this excerpt includes a good amount of information about the literary societies, providing us with a more complete picture. Additionally, it illustrates the growth of this aspect of student life at Haskell.

In the 1897 annual report, Swett does not specifically mention "literary societies," but he was clearly discussing them in the following paragraph:

> This school deserves credit over many other educational institutions from the fact that its pupils are trained to have opinions of their own and to be able to express them in their own language. Among a number of occasions which served to demonstrate this fact our commencement exercises, held June 23, this year, deserve particular mention. Ten of the 32 graduates, upon whom diplomas were conferred on that day, delivered orations on the following topics: "Heroes," "Do the next thing," "The coming woman," "The Indian and education," "The ballot box," "Finish your wreath," "What we owe to others," "The greatest victory," "The teacher and the beautiful," "Individuality." These themes were selected by the speakers themselves, and were treated by them independent of tutorial suggestions. They show an independence of thought and clearness of expression that would do credit to young men and women of a more advanced age and superior education.[83]

Later in this narrative, I discuss briefly the substance of the orations that Swett mentions, but there are some comments to be made on the rest of his entry at this point. First of all, Swett appears to be implying that there were other schools that were not allowing students to "have opinions of their own." Could he be talking about Carlisle? Additionally, his statements about the capabilities of the students give us further evidence of their propensity to embrace the experience.

Based on what we know about the Haskell literary societies so far, like the 18th century literary societies discussed by Horowitz (1987), the Haskell students had a "seriousness of purpose," and they understood that the experience "offered an excellent education for public life." Additionally, entries in *The Indian Leader* indicate that by 1897, Haskell had at least two societies, and they engaged in "lively contest(s)," much like those in mainstream institutions as described by Horowitz. At the same time, as illustrated in the discussion that follows, Haskell had a similar system to that of early high schools (Wetzel, 1905), where each high school "division" was "organized into a literary society" with the exception of the seniors who were "divided into two literary societies, which hold an annual public contest." Likewise, the available information allows me to illuminate commonalities with the societies found in 19th century Black colleges (Little 1980), where the "rhetorical and dramatic talents of their members" were displayed in the presentation of "skits, play, debates and speeches." In other words, the literary societies at 19th century Haskell were equivalent to those found in post-secondary, secondary and minority institutions. And much like the Black literary societies of the early 19th century that contributed to the educational growth of the free Blacks as discussed by Porter (1936), the evidence illustrates that the literary societies at Haskell did indeed provide Native students with opportunities for intellectual growth and knowledge sharing, as well as building character and encouraging democracy. [84]

As one example, evening programs conducted by various classes, especially the upper levels, were held regularly; they gave students a chance to display and hone their oratorical and musical skills. Almost every issue of *The Indian Leader* during the last three years of the 19th century presents references to the programs and a description of the activities—orations, recitations, music performances and solos and presentations—detailing the participants of the various programs.

Even the introduction of electric lights was cause for practice of students' talents:

> The electric lights were turned on in the girls' building for the first time on September 9 [1897], and in the boys' buildings on the 15th. Mrs. Johnson and Mr. Allen thought a celebration was in order, so gave a reception for the double purpose of celebrating the disappearance of the kerosene lamps and to give the employes [sic] and large boys an opportunity of making the acquaintance of the new boys. The reception was certainly very pleasant. An interesting program had been arranged which was successfully carried out. This consisted of music by the band, violin and organ, several songs and a recitation by Elijah Skyman. Both the old pupils and the new enjoyed it very much, as also did the employes [sic]. Delicious fruit of different kinds was served. Some of the old pupils were very earnest in their efforts to get acquainted with the new ones and make them feel at home.[85]

There was also time for acting, as evident in an entry in the March 1898 newspaper that outlines the "February Entertainments":

> Then on Feb. 11 the Commercial class gave their first program, an excellent one from the opening selection by the band to the closing number. "When Women go Voting" called forth shouts of laughter, for when the curtain rose we saw Eddie Swett kneading bread, Judson Peconga doing the family washing and Mike Couture peeling potatoes and rocking the baby. The ladies of the family had gone to the polls to vote and when they came back and found that dinner wasn't ready were very indignant. The great orators, Eddie Swett, Judson Peconga, James Balmer, and M.G. Couture were very entertaining. Eddie Swett's recitation was amusing and well rendered. He received an encore. The song, "The Country Cous-

ins" was well received. Frank Cajune did well in "Rienzi's Address to the Romans;" the "Bairdaphone" as exhibited by the inventor I.H. Baird, received a vigorous encore; Edward Vally sang well; Juanita Espionsa was in good voice and sang "The Flower of Tennessee" very sweetly; the "Old Kentucky Home" was especially well rendered by James Balmer, Frank Cajune, Issac Baird and Edward Vally. In "The Witness" the acting was very good, particularly that of Walter Harris.[86]

This particular entry is an excellent example of the types of activities that consumed the time of students in the higher level classes. It is also an interesting comment on gender relations, as well as social and political awareness.

Other social activities are also portrayed in *The Indian Leader*. For example, the August 1897 issue details a seemingly annual event:

The pupils who are away have probably wondered often if there has been a picnic at the school yet. Well, there has been one and it was a very pleasant one. It was held on July 21, in the afternoon and evening. The weather was just right for a picnic, bright and sunshiny, but not very warm for there was just enough breeze to make one comfortable. Early in the afternoon the boys and girls, large and small, were out on the grounds playing croquet and other games, laughing, talking and enjoying themselves in various ways. About six o'clock, or a little before, the tables were carried from the dining-room into the circle, table cloths spread on and the pretty flowered Japanese napkins put at each plate. Then came the eatables. Such nice large sandwiches, quantities of cheese, pickles, stuffed eggs, cake and apples. Then after the more solid food was eaten the ice cream was served by [female faculty, staff and wives listed] ... Superintendent Swett was here, there, and everywhere directing and helping. Eating in the open air does give people such good appetites; there was nothing to hurry anyone away from the tables, and there was very little food left when all were through. Then without any suggestions from anyone the girls began to wash the dishes. The boys were very gallant and carried dish-water and towels, wiped dishes and assisted until dishes and tables were carried back into the din-ing-room again. The band then played a number of selections, there were more games and much merriment and when the first bugle blew it was hard to say good-night and go in. But it was not long before the grounds were deserted and only a few napkins blowing about, and numerous apple cores, remained to show that the July picnic had taken place.[87]

The scene is well accounted for and actually very idyllic right up to the sound of the bugle. This is an example of how regimentation was never too far removed from the students at 19th century Haskell.

One particular entry in a November 1898 issue of *The Indian Leader* illustrates an imaginative approach on the part of the hospital cook, Ella F. Cooper, who found an inventive way to get students to partici-pate in a mundane chore.

The Contest.

There have been several oratorical contests at Haskell, as well as contests in spelling, arithmetic, marching and athletic sports, but the first bean shelling contest was held on Saturday evening, October 22. Mrs. Cooper originated the idea and issued the invitations.

What a merry time the contestants had. Their hands were busy but that did not prevent their tongues from working. Those engaged in the contest were Anna Lockwood, Eliza Marmon, Esther Brien, Edith Sharp, Jennie Chapman, Addie Wise, Jessie McLoud, May Long, Laura Taylor, Susie Crowe, Anna Crane, Mamie Setter, Alma Poole, Rose Tredo, Charlie Wright, Charlie Jennison, Allen Crane, John Holland, Willie Weller, Roy Jones, James Norris and Charlie Roubidoux.

After shelling forty minutes the bell was tapped for work to stop. The beans were measured and Jessie McLoud was declared the winner of the large toothsome cake, decorated with candy beans of different colors, as she had shelled 2 ¾ pints of beans. Roy Jones received the booby prize, "Jack and the Beanstalk and Other Stories." His beans measured 1/3 of a pint. Jessie very generously divided her cake with her friends and Ray is ready to read from his book to all who wish to hear about "Jack," "Cinderella," and the other interesting characters whose histories are given.

Mrs. Cooper, assisted by her daughter, Miss Bertha and Miss Grace Dixon, then served refreshments consisting of buttered rolls, pressed meat, pickles, tarts, frosted doughnuts and cake. Games followed; the one most enjoyed was picking up potatoes on a teaspoon and placing them in a dish. Edith Sharp and Charlie Jennison were the captains. Edith's side was victorious, winning in nine out of eleven trials with the two rows of stubborn potatoes that seemed determined to go everywhere else but on the spoons.[88]

This illustrates the creativity of at least one individual on the Haskell staff. The invitations would make it appealing, like a party was in the works. Then the first prize of a cake would whet the appetite of those asked to participate. It was also an opportunity to socialize, probably valued among the students. Ultimately, the bean-shucking contest was an intelligent approach to a dreaded task, as least as far as the cook was concerned. Perhaps the students who had to shuck the beans would not agree with the positive portrayal of this undoubtedly monotonous task. In any case, now I would like to turn the attention to the classroom experience of the 19th century Haskell students.

Instruction

A key aspect of survival was learning academic basics in the classrooms. To look at this, I turn to some of the educational experiences of Haskell students in the 1890s. Naturally, there appears to be no direct evidence of this aspect from the 1880s, but there is information that allows stories to be told about the last five years of the 19th century.

Before moving into my discussion of the normal and commercial departments, I first review basic progression of higher level learning within the institution. When Haskell first opened in 1884, students were provided with instruction in grades levels one through five. The students were taught to speak English, and they studied math, geography, and other academic subjects as would be necessary in everyday life. There was also instruction in areas such as cooking, sewing, laundry, baking, carpentry, masonry, and farming—all subjects of industrial education.

Second in size only to Carlisle, Haskell was one of seven off-reservation industrial schools in 1894, ten years after it opened. In the fall of that year, the Normal Department (teacher training) and kindergarten were introduced at the suggestion of Superintendent of Indian Schools, William Hailmann. One year later, in 1895, a Commercial Department was added. It was in 1896, under Superintendent Swett, when Haskell's literary or Academic Department was expanded to include eleven graded class divisions along with the Commercial and Normal Departments.[89] Although there were at least three other normal schools in the off-reservation boarding schools operating from 1894 to 1901, it appears that Haskell was the only institution with a Commercial Department. This suggests that by the end of the 19th century, Haskell was the premier institution in the government-operated Indian school system; in strictly educational terms, it surpassed all of the other like institutions.

Certainly, the students at Haskell were still subject to all of the harsh realities of boarding school life with the goal of assimilation; however, the literary and social structures appear to be a gentler method of inculcation of dominant society. The Normal Department began producing teachers, while the Commercial Department was generating clerks, typists, and stenographers, as well as potential entrepreneurs and business people. A few students went on to mainstream colleges, including the University of Kansas, after graduation from Haskell.

Meanwhile, the social structure for the older students at Haskell appears to have loosely resembled the college life of a student in a main-stream or black institution of higher education and the student life in at least some high schools. The literary societies, glee clubs, Y.M.C.A., and athletics that were all active at Haskell during the final five years of the 1890s mirrored the activities taking place at the time on college and high schools campuses across the country. Ultimately, although some degree of student life can be found in other levels, it was in the Normal and Commercial Departments where the bulk of the student activity took place. With that in mind, the focus of this narrative now turns to the Normal School, beginning with a discussion of the impetus behind its success.

The Normal Department

According to the annual report filed by Superintendent Swett in 1895, following the 1894–1895 school year, the kindergarten and Normal Department at Haskell were established as the result of a suggestion by Superintendent of Indian Schools, William Hailmann:

> The normal class was organized in October, with 4 boys and 7 girls as members. These students, all of whom had completed the grammar-school course, took up the normal work with enthusiasm and successfully completed the first year's work at the end of the school year. Although this department was not well equipped, the results attained are of a very satisfactory character, and prove beyond a doubt that these young people are capable and may with proper training become successful teachers.

The addition of the kindergarten class was not only "in itself a success, but it has been of great value as a model department, in which the students of the normal department have made observation and taken training in kindergarten methods."[90] In very real terms, the 1894–1895 school year brought a higher level of learning to the students at Haskell.

Hailmann (1899), in a discussion of the introduction of normal school programs at off-reservation industrial schools in the year after he left the position of Superintendent of Indian Schools, wrote:

> With a view of training teachers systematically and in greater number for the work of teaching, the government in 1894 added to three of these [seven] schools normal departments. This was done at Carlisle, at the Haskell institute and at Santa Fe, and these schools were henceforth distinguished as industrial and normal training schools. The experiment proved fairly successful with Carlisle where, indeed, similar work had been previously done, and, more especially, with the Haskell institute. The school at Santa Fe during the first years accomplished little in this direction, but of late has begun to gain success under a gifted superintendent.[91]

Hailmann's statement corroborates how Haskell surpassed even Carlisle in the educational arena. As stated earlier, one of the reasons this endeavor was more successful at Haskell was due to the educational backgrounds of the men in charge and their desire to make it work.

In his 1896 annual report, Haskell Superintendent Swett deviated from the past protocol of providing tables of the number of tribes represented at Haskell, as well as the totals of items produced by students as a result of their industrial work. Instead, Swett augmented his report with a table that classified students according to grade level, noting,

> This report as compared with other classification reports shows an advancement in scholarship of the students . . . The increase in attendance, as shown by the annual statistical report, and the gradual raising of the standard of scholarship, as shown by the classification report, are encouraging features of the past year's record, and demonstrate that the benefits of more thorough education and training are being appreciated by Indian people as never before.[92]

Although the commercial department had just been introduced during the previous school year, there were twenty males and six females enrolled. Meanwhile, the number of normal class students remained at eleven, the same number as the year before, with six males and five females enrolled. Clearly, Swett spent more time discussing the academic pursuits of the institution than any previous superintendent had done; the prior leaders had focused on the industrial accomplishments of the institution—how many wagons or shirts were produced, and how many bushels of corn or beans were grown by the students.

Swett's 1897 annual report illustrates a shift in the interests of the students; the attendance in the Commercial Department had dropped to eighteen total, while the Normal Department swelled to include twenty-three students. The former graduated its first class of seven, while the latter had four graduates. Of the Normal School graduates, Swett wrote, "with a number of years' experience in public-school work and among public-school teachers, I can say emphatically that in mental attainments and skill in teaching they are superior to many who go forth as teachers in our public schools."[93]

Not only did Superintendent Swett have faith in the normal graduates, he also wanted his superiors to know what he thought about Haskell students and the education they received at the institution in general. As quoted earlier, Swett wrote in his 1897 annual report: "This school deserves credit over many other educational institutions from the fact that its pupils are trained to have opinions of their own and to be able to express them in their own language." At the risk of being repetitive, I offer this again to portray the superintendent's convictions. As proof of the abilities of his students, Swett shared the titles of the orations delivered at commencement that year by ten graduating students, including "The Coming Woman," "The Indian and Education," "The Ballot Box," and "What We Owe to Others." The superintendent then clarified that the orations "were selected by the speakers themselves and were treated by them independent of tutorial suggestions." Swett further extolled the virtues of the orations when he declared that the orations showed "an independence of thought and clearness of expression that would do credit to young men and women of a more advanced age and superior education."[94]

Meanwhile, in his 1897 annual report, Captain Pratt of Carlisle illustrated his feeling toward Haskell when he wrote:

> We do not give a normal diploma, like some younger institutions, nor do we have a commercial course aside from the general bookkeeping and common business forms; but when our students can go into State normal schools and into the commercial institutions in Carlisle and elsewhere and take diplomas from them, they get what is far more significant as a means of entering the army of teachers and business men and women of the land than anything that can be given in the best Indian or purely racial school.[95]

Pratt, a military man with a third-grade education, thought "higher education" should be left to the mainstream institutions, largely because he had little faith in the educational abilities of Indian students as a whole. Fortunately, this belief was not one shared by the educators at Haskell.

Although it is difficult to assess the first two years of Haskell's normal department due to the lack of available references, that would change in March, 1897, with the introduction of the campus newspaper *The Indian Leader*. Although the periodical was only printed once a month during the first two years, in 1899 it was printed every other week and beginning in 1900, it became a weekly. As a source of information, *The Indian Leader* is rich in substance once a researcher looks beyond the white-influenced moral stories and those of the "bad Indian gone good," and other concerted efforts of assimilation through story. It is in this periodical that I find solid references to the inner circle of Haskell's Normal Department. At the same time, I find multiple examples of an active student life at 19th century Haskell.

It appears that the issue referred to in Pratt's comment infers a question of quality. In order to determine the quality of Haskell's Normal

Department, it is useful to compare it with like public institutions of the time. This is possible with a recently released text that details the history of the state normal schools in the United States. *The American State Normal School: "An Instrument of Great Good,"* by Christine A. Ogren, provides a comprehensive view of the topic (2005).

The first state normal schools were established in Massachusetts in 1839. In Kansas, the first state normal school was established in 1865 at Emporia. It was from this institution, Emporia State Teachers College, that the fifth superintendent of Haskell, Hervey B. Peairs, graduated in 1887, a few months before he was hired at Haskell as a first and second grade teacher.

There was some form of teacher training to be found in various academies and colleges prior to the rise and during the heyday of the state normal schools; some institutions established normal departments and some included normal classes in the curriculum. A normal department was established at the University of Kansas in 1876; however, like many other normal departments in other state universities in the Midwest, it was short-lived.

By 1890, there were 103 state normal schools "located in 35 (of 44) states, as well as Arizona Territory." According to Ogren, "The revolutionary spark of the early normal schools ignited during the institutions' heyday between the 1870s and the 1900s . . . Also during this period, normal schools began to educate members of racial minority groups, both in separate institutions and in majority-white schools."[96] It is evident that Superintendent of Indian Schools Hailmann, and perhaps Haskell Superintendent Swett as well, was aware of this movement and decided that Haskell was ready to keep up with the national trend. Additionally, the Native teachers could be sent into the reservation schools to help spread the message of civilization.

In the late 19th century state normal schools, the curriculum was not as expansive as that found in the institutions of higher education across the country, but the structure of the curriculum at most normal schools throughout this period provided the foundation for a vibrant intellectual life on campus. Work in academic subjects fostered reasoning powers, analytical skills, and interest in intellectual matters, while academic requirements ensured that students gained exposure to a range of subjects and that all students studied the same core of "substantial branches of learning."[97] Of the Normal Department at Haskell, Hailmann wrote in 1899:

> The normal course, planned for two years, deals with the rudiments of algebra and geometry, with elementary physics, general history, rhetoric, American and English literature, and—on the professional side—with psychology, history of pedagogy, pedagogics, discussion of methods, and practice teaching under the direction of a critic teacher . . . Graduates of the normal department are offered the opportunity to devote one additional year to preparation for kindergarten work under the direction of the kindergartner of the institution, and in connection with a well-equipped kindergarten, where they are permitted to observe the work and occasionally to assist in it.[98]

Hailmann's description of Haskell's curriculum does not seem too far removed from Ogren's general discussion regarding the curriculum in state normal schools that included "required classes in mathematics, the sciences, history, and English language arts" to develop "students' reasoning and analytical skills as well as their abilities to express their ideas, while optional advanced studies presented the opportunity to acquire prestigious cultural knowledge."[99]

As normal departments and teachers' classes flourished at higher learning institutions during the mid- 19th century, graduation became a production of sorts: "At the elaborate commencement ceremonies in which each graduating student presented an oration, essay or declamation, it became very common for one or more students to address an educational topic."[100] It was no different at Haskell.

At the June 20, 1897, Haskell commencement exercises, a number of students graduating from the normal, commercial, or preparatory classes gave orations. The texts presented by the students were printed in *The Indian Leader*. At the ceremony, two brothers were the orators of the graduating Commercial Department class: John V. Plake presented "The Ballot Box," a piece about the privilege of voting and James W. Plake's "Finish Your Wreath" relates first to the Athenian days when victors were crowned with laurel wreaths, and then describes the need for individuals to build their own wreaths out of integrity, honesty, honor and other like qualities.[101]

Four members of the Normal Department class also presented their work: George Shawnee's piece, "Individuality," focused on utilizing and expanding one's intellectual capabilities; Jerdie Dawson discussed admirable attributes desirable in an educator in "The Teacher and the Beautiful"; Nellie Wright, in "The Greatest Victory," also discussed the importance of teaching, concluding that "if pupils are led to conquer, or master their passions, temper, desires, appetites, feelings, and un-worthy ambitions, they have won the greatest victory ever won"; and Rose Dougherty's piece, "What We Owe to Others," described the virtues of civilization for the Indian, utilizing as examples, Pestalozzi's Gertrude, Francke and Booker T. Washington.[102]

There were also four members of the Senior Grammar School class who presented their work. Sadie Merris's "Do Ye the Next Thing" dis-cussed will power and persistence with General Grant as an example; Eliza Patelle's presentation, "The Coming Woman," briefly described the necessary advancement of women utilizing Lucy Stone, Susan B. An-thony and Frances E. Willard as cases in point; William M. Plake's "He-roes" discussed the issue in general terms with Washington and Grant as examples; and finally, Frank Shaw's text, "The Indian and Education," discussed the necessity of formal education for Native youth.[103]

Based on the caliber of the material presented, it seems that this graduation line-up would be considered equivalent to the types of orations that took place in the state normal schools' commencements. Additionally, it says something about the education of the 19th century Haskell students. The themes include voting, civilization and "white" icons—all American societal values.

From time to time, *The Indian Leader* would print an essay in its entirety; more often, there would be references to the titles of the ora-tions and the speaker. The three upper-level classes had presentations on a regular basis. Meanwhile, in the state normal schools, according to Ogren, "in addition to honing their skills in analysis, these assignments to compose essays on literature refined students' writing skills." Ogren goes on to observe: "Indeed, the main focus in the English curricula at state normal schools was the expression of ideas in both writing and speech ... Most normal schools required each student to present some sort of school-wide public declamation at least once, but often on a weekly or monthly basis."[104] Again, Haskell appears to be in keeping with the state normal schools of the time.

Literary societies were also an aspect of state normal schools. Although these societies began giving way to Greek letter fraternities in colleges and universities in the 1870s, "at the state normal schools between the 1870s and the 1900s, however, the literary societies could not have been more integral to student life."[105] Haskell Superintendent Swett mentions "several well organized literary societies and Christian organizations did splendid work all through the year" in his 1894 annual report. As stated earlier, this appears to be the first reference to literary societies in the annual reports filed by the Haskell Superintendents.[106]

Societies are, however, mentioned in the first issue of *The Indian Leader*. "The joint meeting of the two literary societies was held last evening. James Whitcomb Riley was the poet whose works were studied during the month and the program was largely made up of selections from the Indiana poet."[107] The program listed includes both male and female names, so it is unclear if there was one society for each sex or if they were both co-educational. In October, 1898, there was an expansion from two to four literary societies, two male and two female.[108] All four societies remained active through the turn of the century, serving as extra-curricular activities for the upper level students.

Another similarity between state normal schools and Haskell in the last part of the 1800s was in the use of social spaces. Of state normal schools, their population and social spaces, Ogren (2005) writes:

Normalites created their own tradition of more- and less-formal events in which women and men were equally active and visible . . . The capstone of each year's social as well as intellectual life, graduating festivities included "class days." Fairly widespread by the 1890s, class-day exercises varied somewhat from school to school. Generally, students of both sexes took the stage to read the class history and prophesy . . . Oshkosh's class days in the late 1880s and early 1890s included humorous "botanical" and "zoological" analyses of the seniors, and Castleton's in the late 1890s included addresses to the juniors that offered advice as well as gentle gibes.[109]

At Haskell, versions of these types of activities were evident. Early in Elijah Brown's story, there is an example of this, where the upper class bequeaths something to the lower class and Elijah responds for the latter. As another example, the Commencement 1897 issue of *The Indian Leader* includes details of "A Pleasant Reception":

> A very pleasant reception was given on last Friday evening by some of the young men. It was held in the dining hall but the familiar place wore an unfamiliar look. The tables were all moved out of the central part of the hall which was changed into a cosy [sic] parlor by the many rugs, rocking chairs and tables. A short program was given. The regular numbers were: song, Junior Normal boys; "The Chariot Race," Elijah Skyman; vocal solo; Miss Robbins; Class History, James Vandal.[110]

The informal gathering of the junior Normal Department class is in keeping with what was happening in state normal schools during the same time frame.

In the same 1897 commencement issue is printed "Class Prophecy," which shares one student's futuristic forecast for the commercial class. It begins, "One morning in June 1917, I received a letter addressed in a neat hand which appeared to me had been written with the muscular movement such as I learned while attending the Business Department at Haskell. At that moment my mind wandered back to the year 1897, but coming to my senses, as it were, I opened the letter."[111] Although the prophecy is done for the commercial and not the normal class, it is a telling illustration of the fact that Haskell had many of the same types of social interactions as similar dominant society institutions.

In the end, it appears that the students in the upper-level departments—normal, commercial and preparatory—all had access to a type of student life that was characteristic of the time. There is very little information about the literary societies specifically, but it appears obvious that these organizations were intricately intertwined with the upper level departments. Therefore, the societies were not treated in isolation, but rather as extensions of their departments. Likewise, there is little specific information about the musical organizations in the early years. Instead, the information is sprinkled within the text of *The Indian Leader,* although we do know that the Haskell band was a success, a point mentioned by other authors. While the Normal Department was busy growing and keeping up with the national trends, there was also growth in another educational area of Haskell, the Commercial Department, my next point of discussion.

The Commercial Department

While this study does not delve too deeply into the history of the Commercial Department, it is necessary to give some measure of the department in order to fully assess Captain Pratt's appraisal of the higher levels of learning at an Indian school. The commercial department was the alternative choice for the upper level students. Like those in the normal school, students in this department were engaged in active student lives in addition to their educational pursuits.

The first mention of the Commercial Department is in the second issue of *The Indian Leader,* printed in April, 1897. In a specifically designated and titled section, the paper states that the department had nineteen students—sixteen male and three female. The students won "first and second places in thought and composition" in the oratorical contest that included representatives from the normal class, the commercial, and the ninth grade (preparatory) class; and "a new type-writing and dictation room has been added which will be of great advantage to the classes in shorthand, typewriting and mimeograph work." These entries provide a little bit of background on the department.

Another separate entry on the same page refers to a Haskell commercial department item that was reprinted from another publication:

> The March number of the "Stenographer" says: Mr. C.C. See-wir, of the Haskell Institute, Lawrence, Kansas, says, that "of a shorthand class of six Indian boys and girls, after nine months study, all of them, with but one exception, can write from 60 to 80 words per minute." He adds: "When it is taken into consideration what is to be overcome in the Indian youth we, out here, think it pretty fair work." These same pupils can now write from 90 to 110 words per minute.[112]

The final sentence appears to be an indication that at least five of the students in the class had progressed and their shorthand skills had increased in a month's time by thirty words per minute. That would seem to be a fair gain.

Also on the same page of the April, 1897, issue of *The Indian Leader* is a story about the "second oratorical contest," which includes further information about four members of the 1897 commercial class in separate entries. Presented in the order of their delivery—although there were orations from other students between them—the entries read as follows:

> George Bent of the commercial class, was the first speaker. His oration was earnest and showed careful preparation. His subject was "The Trident of Success."
>
> The oration which was awarded the highest grade by the judges in thought and composition was the one by John V. Plake of the senior commercial class upon "Partisan and Citizen." Mr. Plake has certainly spent much thought upon this subject; not only this, the thoughts were well expressed in clear well rounded sentences.

One of the strongest orations of the evening was given by James W. Plake of the senior commercial class. His subject was "Exterminate the Indian but Leave the Man." Mr. Plake knew his oration perfectly but just before going on the stage to make assurance doubly sure he glanced over it once more. This in some way confused him and caused him to leave out a portion of the carefully prepared, thoughtful discourse. With this exception his delivery was fine, his manner dignified and impressive.

One of the most earnest, thoughtful orations was Isaac Baird's. Mr. Baird was one of the representatives of the commercial class. His manner was quiet and unaffected. His subject was "Beacon Lights of the World."[113]

What is interesting in this set of entries is the description of James Plake's actions in presenting his text. Was James really confused and consequently left out a portion of his presentation, or is it possible that he deliberately sabotaged his performance knowing that John, his younger brother, had the winning production without his competition? The idealist would concur with the latter, as I do.

The May 1897 issue of *The Indian Leader* provides further information about the status of the Commercial Department in two entries:

The Senior shorthand class are putting all the extra time in practicing for speed in order to be able to write 120 words a minute, which is the number of words required for graduation.

On April 27 both the Seniors and Juniors visited the Lawrence Business College in town, and found that most of the text books were the same as are used at our school.[114]

As the focus of this study is not on the Commercial Department specifically, and so extensive research has not been done in that area, it is unknown if these two entries provide an adequate measure of success as a department. In other words, it is unclear if 120 words a minute was a standard for other similar, mainstream institutions, nor is the standing of Lawrence Business College known. However, the entries certainly seem to provide some measure of Haskell's Commercial Department for consideration.

An entry in "Commercial Notes" in the November, 1897, issue provides an amusing example of assimilation in learning:

> The Commercials have formed a Research Club. Each member chose or was given a topic to look up and report on in a meeting to be held on Friday, Nov. 5. The subject under discussion is, materials used in connection with, and history of ironing."[115]

Perhaps this entry is not the best example of higher learning at 19th century Haskell, but it does indicate that certain topics were pursued in considerable depth. The February, 1898, commercial column states: "The Junior class completed the work in Commercial Law in nearly three weeks less than the allotted time with a class average of 91¾ per cent."[116] Again, the value of the course is unclear; however, the entry illuminates progressive Haskell students. In March 1898, "The Commercial class paid a very enjoyable visit to the Lawrence Business College . . . The work of the actual business department was particularly observed. After leaving the Business College, a short visit was paid to the University."[117]

By 1900, it is obvious that the commercial department is flourishing, as evidenced by this entry in *The Indian Leader*:

> That the pen is mightier than the tomahawk is shown in the package of specimens of excellent business writing received from the students of the Indian School, Haskell Institute, Lawrence, Kansas. This writing represents the every-day class work of the students in the commercial department of this institution, under the instruction of C.E. Birch. Mr. Birch is entitled to extra credit, and no doubt the students are also, for the excellent showing made, as the writing is much better than

the average writing of white students in business colleges.—
Penman's Art Journal, New York.[118]

In other words, it appears that the students engaged in study in Haskell's
Commercial Department were operating at a high level, even beyond
the students in similar mainstream institutions. One may ask—How
is this possible? For one thing, the instructors at 19th century Haskell
Institute obviously had faith in the capabilities of their students, contributing to the faith of the students in themselves. Secondly, I must
consider the role of outside influences, and one in particular. There can
be no doubt that the university on the hill definitely had an influence
on 19th century Haskell Institute. It is some indication of that influence
that constitutes the final subject in my narrative.

The University of Kansas Connection

It can be assumed that some of the progress made at Haskell is due
to its proximity to the state university that sat prominently on Mount
Oread. As stated earlier, the social aspects of the higher grade levels
at Haskell loosely resembled the burgeoning student life emerging at
college campuses across the country.

Indeed, there is ample evidence of a connection between Haskell
Institute and the University of Kansas (KU) during the 19th century.
For example, James Marvin, who was KU's Chancellor from 1874–
1883, served as the first superintendent of Haskell, 1884–1885. Additionally, KU Chancellor Joshua Lippincott (1883–1889) gave the
opening address when Haskell was officially opened in the fall of 1884.
Lippincott moved to Lawrence from Carlisle, Pennsylvania, where he
had been employed as a professor of mathematics at Dickinson College; like Marvin before him, Lippincott was a clergyman. In fact, Lippincott previously served three years as a chaplain at Carlisle.[119]

In addition to instituting an expanded course of study, Superintendent Swett, in 1896, sought out the valuable resource located up
the hill. It is noted in his 1896 annual report that the normal class included lectures by KU professors. Although Swett does not elaborate,

the introduction of *The Indian Leader* in March of 1897 allows one a small glimpse of the types of lectures and the professors who delivered them. The first blurb regarding the lectures appears in the second issue, "Prof. Bailey, of the State University, gave a very interesting lecture last evening on 'Air.' The excellent talk was illustrated with many experiments which delighted as well as instructed the young people."[120] In the following month, May, 1897, there was a lecture held every Friday for three weeks:

> Prof. Sayre, of the State University, gave an entertaining and profitable lecture to the pupils Friday evening, April 9. His subject was "Color." The experiments were greatly enjoyed.
>
> Professor Miller gave a very entertaining and instructive lecture on Friday evening, April 23. His subject was "The Starry Heavens." The views shown were also helpful as well as beautiful.
>
> Professor Blackmar's illustrated lecture on April 16, was much enjoyed. The subject was "Spanish Missions." The Haskell employes [sic] and pupils consider themselves very fortunate to have the privilege of listening to so many able and cultured men as are on the lecture course this season. We are certainly very grateful to these gentlemen for their kindness.[121]

It is obvious that even some of the less advanced students took note of the lectures, even if they didn't quite comprehend the content.

For example, although it is not clear when the lecture took place, a June, 1897, entry in *The Indian Leader* illustrates the efforts of some students to incorporate their lecture learning into their writing: "The Third Primary pupils were using abbreviations in sentences the other day. One was this, 'Prof. Dyche killed some icebergs.'" Another was, "'Prof. Dyche went nearly to the North Post.'"[122] Obviously, Professor Dyche had lectured at Haskell on a trip he took to the North Pole. These examples serve to illustrate connections between Haskell Institute, a government-run boarding school with assimilation-through-education goals and the University of Kansas, a state-sponsored institution of higher education, a benefit to the 19th century Haskell students.

Hailmann took note of this relationship in an assessment of Haskell in 1899. He wrote:

The fact that the Kansas state university is located at Lawrence exerts a stimulating influence upon the institution. The professors of the university take an active personal interest in its welfare and favor it from time to time with courses of lectures adapted to the needs of the pupils. As a result the desire grows in their hearts to secure for themselves university training after graduating from Haskell. At present there are two graduates of the institution in the law school of the university.[123]

Hailmann may have wished for desire from the Native students in embracing the higher levels of learning available at the school up the hill; however, whether the non-Native students in the school up the hill were ready to embrace the Native students or not during the last decades of the 1800s was another matter.

Obviously, the Lawrence community supported the Haskell Institute—the local citizens did raise almost $10,000 to purchase the original 280 acres of land the institution occupied, and later they did raise money for band equipment when Charles Robinson asked for their assistance in bringing culture to Haskell's campus. And, for the most part, it appears that individuals at KU were eager to assist in the education process of the Native youth. One example of this type of behavior can be found in the May, 1897, issue of *The Indian Leader*:

A Young Women's Christian Association has just been organized at the school. On Wednesday, April 14, three young ladies from the University came out and a meeting was held to talk of organizing a Y.W.C.A. The girls were greatly interested and before the meeting closed it was decided that the young ladies should come again the next Wednesday evening and organize the society. At the next meeting the association was further discussed and two committees were appointed, one on nominations and one on constitution. The following Wednesday the officers were elected, the constitution adopted, and the organization of the Y.W.C.A. of Haskell Institute was completed. The officers elected were as follows: President, Josephine Armstrong; vice president, Edith Sharp; corresponding secretary Ida Robinson; recording secretary, Nellie Wright; treasurer, Rose Daugherty; Miss Laura Radford, the state secretary, presided over the last meeting. She talked very earnestly to the girls and resolves were made that, by the help of God, the Y.W.C.A. of Haskell Institute should become a power for Him.[124]

Although I might conclude that the only reason the young ladies participated was because they were doing their Christian duty, it does indicate willingness of various factions to engage in some type of relationship with the Native students of Haskell. To witness the opposite end of the spectrum, a researcher need look no further than the Senior Annuals produced by the upper-level students at KU.

There were only five annuals printed between 1873 and 1889. One of these annuals, *The Cicala*, was published in 1884, just about the time the Haskell campus was beginning to take shape. The publication includes a short one-act play, meant to be a comedy, but steeped with Native stereotypes:

> Indian Industrial School
> In the quiet valley which lies at the foot of Mount Oread, and far to the southward, the wise men of state agreed to erect a school for Indian youth, the second in the United States. There, situated on a rise in the valley, its massive gray walls rise as though in rivalry of those grand old structures on Mt. Oread. That is the home of the young braves and squaws of the land. O mighty Fathers! How farseeing your wisdom! How fitting a place!—Lawrence, with its theatres, libraries and culture, for the assimilation of the dusky one of the for-

est! Already the work of conversion has begun. The irrepressible Senior, with his mortar-board, and the Soph, with his insurmountable cheek, were the first to catch the eye of the dusky maid.

Reader, have you ever looked metaphysically into the relations existing between cause and effect? If so, you are prepared to witness the following:

[SCENE: *University campus, on the south.* Senior, *lying under the shade of a friendly oak, quietly smoking a cigarette. Approach* Indian Maiden, *gathering flowers on the hillside. Approach, at the same time,* Senior.]

SENIOR: O sweet Corn-Bread Bess, light of my eyes!

CORN-BREAD BESS: *Schemocman yalle! Heap good.*

SENIOR: O heavenly creature, "more fair than light from Eden's streams," I adore you!—

CORN-BREAD BESS: *Ugh! Pawpa wooqua peasah! Ne *piasa? Heap cough?*

SENIOR (*forking over the ever present curative and preventative*): Nymph of the valley, will you accompany me to hear the far-famed warbler Abbott?

CORN-BREAD BESS: *Heap Eli! Blingee hack. Ice Cleamee. Yalle! Yalle!*

————

*Fire-water[125]

The grunts and broken English, the fire-water, the braves and squaws, all are images or tags that have been seemingly permanently attached to the Native Peoples—they were in use then and they are used still today.

On the facing page of this misguided comedy, a further insult is served:

Indian Industrial School.

FACULTY.★
[ONE GENERATION HENCE.]

LAUGH-AT-HIS-SHADOW CANFIELD, JR.,
PRESIDENT.
Professor of Gymnastics and Overseer of the Laundry.

OLD-MAN-ON-HIS-EAR ROBINSON, JR.,
Professor of Horse-Shoeing and Morals.

BUG-ON-HIS-NOSE SNOW, JR.
Professor of Coon-Skinning and Esthetics.

BRIMSTONE BAILEY, JR.
Manufacturer of Fire-Water and General Healer.

SIT-ON-THE-BRAVES CARRUTH, JR.
Overseer of Hash and Prayers.

BLOOD-IN-HIS-EYE SPRING, JR.
Curator of the Happy Hunting Grounds.

STAR-IN-HIS-HAND NICHOLS, JR.,
Guider of the Heavenly Spears.

BLIND-IN-ONE-EYE BROWNELL, JR.,
Instructor in War-Whoops and Theology.

SCOWLS-AT-THE-BRAVES LIPPINCOTT, JR.,
In Charge of Tobacco Supply.

STICK-IN-THE-MUD WILLIAMS, JR.,
Missionary and Blacksmith.

———

★Word for word as given by the Sibyl of North Lawrence.
We decline assuming any responsibility for its accuracy.—
EDS[126]

All of the surnames utilized in the preceding listing correspond with surnames of professors listed in the actual faculty listing included in the beginning pages of the annual.

Although the content of the annual was intended to induce humor, it obviously would have been offensive to people of Native descent, not just because of the derogatory nature of the stereotypes, but more importantly, because of the deprecating references to aspects considered spiritual or sacred in the Native cultures. Native peoples dared not take aspects such as healers, tobacco, and the "happy hunting grounds" lightly. Granted, I can be fairly sure that few, if any, Native individuals actually had access to this annual and its twisted comedy. But even so, what purpose did it serve in furthering racist attitudes toward the race it belittled? Ultimately, it could have contributed to preconceived notions that non-Native students held of any Native students who eventually did go on to face the challenges of life on Mount Oread.

PART IV: CONCLUSION--SURVIVIAL

In the end, the stories in this chapter illustrate the fact that despite the many challenges present at 19th century Haskell, some students thrived and gained a solid education. Additionally, the stories highlight, to some extent, the opportunities that were available at 19th century Haskell. Even though, like high schools, the student life at the school was not created by the students but rather by the teachers, the stories included in this narrative demonstrate that students embraced it and made it their own. Perhaps Vuckovic says it best:

> The children adapted to the circumstances and compensated for the institution's deficiencies with their great sense of community, friendship, and compassion. What the school could not provide for them, they successfully provided for each other: emotional warmth and mutual care. Haskell could only survive because the children appropriated the school for their own needs. They transformed it into their own world, a truly Indian school that meant more to them than educators had ever envisioned.[127]

In other words, the students adapted to the environment first, then found ways to adapt components of the environment to suit them. They found a way to embrace the good and accept the bad. They found a way to survive.

Other Stories Waiting to Be Told

Various authors have portrayed the history of Haskell during the late 1800s. The earliest documents portray the institution always from the top down, rarely reaching the student perspective. The most recent documents, however, lend balance to the older, heavily biased texts. At least two authors, Anderson and Vuckovic, have done an admirable job of detailing the reality of the Haskell student perspective during the earliest years. Even so, all of the texts produced about Haskell focus on many of the same issues, usually including the perspective, directly and indirectly, of the administration. Although at least two of the narratives do include some student perspectives, these insights are isolated within a specific category of analysis. In the end, what is missing in historical Haskell studies are the stories of the students themselves. As can be seen in this narrative, in spite of the meager resources, there are still many student connections that can be identified. In this way it is possible to glimpse their lives.

The foregoing text has been produced with the intent of answering the initial questions—What are the stories of the students at 19th century Haskell and where are they told? The stories told do not necessarily reflect the average student's experience at Haskell Institute in the early years, yet they do provide a deeper understanding of the experience of a handful of individuals who lived and learned there in the late 19th century.

Some of these stories tell of students who suffered loss—Ada Mahojah, Vincent Sears and George Eberhald all lost siblings. Julius Caesar, Napoleon Bonaparte and Andrew Jackson lost their identity. Thomas Tuttle and Josiah Patterson lost their lives. These students all made sacrifices. But there were also sacrifices made by all the early Haskell students. Many of them sacrificed time with their families. Some sacrificed their health. All sacrificed their culture to some degree, even if only for a time.

But there are also many stories of survival—James and Johnnie Plake, who essentially grew up at Haskell, embraced what was offered to them; ultimately, they excelled in aspects of their student life at Haskell, and they went on to live successful lives. They learned how to survive. And of course, there is the ultimate story of survival, in my eyes—Elijah Brown, the young man who lost a limb, but who not only persevered, but went on to become an upstanding member of the community. He, too, embraced the good and accepted the bad; he learned how to survive.

When looked at from this perspective, it could be said that Haskell was a survival school. Survival skills were learned in the literary societies, the Normal School and the Commercial Department. At the same time, students were gaining different survival skills in the Sewing Department and on the farm. They were acquiring skills that would allow them to survive in a world quite different from their own.

Altogether, these stories illustrate student life at Haskell Institute in the 19th century. This text is evidence that there are stories that can provide access to experiences of some Haskell students. Horowitz (1987) describes student life as "worlds (that) give form to students' lives and meaning to their experience."[128] It was no different at Haskell. Like students in higher-level institutions across the country, Haskell students created their own worlds. Of course, there were many more limitations for them, but in spaces like the literary societies, they determined what form their experience would take. Furthermore, in a world of strict rules and little freedom, students were able to exercise some control over their lives, even if only in the simple act of choosing and developing their topics of investigation and oratory.

Actually, as I look beyond the negative aspects of boarding school life, I can say that Haskell had much of the best of college life. For one thing, the literary societies operated in a traditional way, meaning the students approached their tasks in a serious, academic manner. Secondly, there was no need to worry about fraternities and all the social problems attached to them. Finally, there were no divisions between rich and poor. Common dividers such as clothing or material possessions were not an issue at an institution where uniforms were issued and money was minimal. Meanwhile, the band and athletic teams were quickly gaining status for the school.

In addition to providing a "new" history of 19th century Haskell Institute, the stories presented in this document also provide information about the institution and boarding schools, as well as the larger social and political environment. Patriotism, Christianity and Victorian values, as well as assimilation and allotment goals, were embedded within the student life at Haskell. This is representative of the "education for civilization" that was present in all boarding schools. These stories illustrate that students actively pursued that education and succeeded.

It has not been an easy task to construct stories of a marginalized group from over a century ago. But careful research can uncover some fragmentary stories of individuals who once marched across the same campus where I now walk. My research uncovers stories of forgotten students and raises a multitude of questions at the same time. Research has answered the opening questions. I now know that some of the stories are buried in obscure documents and a periodical.

There are more stories waiting to be constructed. As for me, I have discovered more stories than I could begin to imagine when I started this project. Of course, they are only small bits and pieces of individual and collective stories. And of course, there is room for error in my interpretation of the various documents, as well as in the question of accuracy of the documents themselves. But in the end, I share stories of student sacrifice and survival that have not been told in previous narratives. These are valuable stories, even if only small remnants. Their value lies in their ability to illustrate some of the sacrifices made by the early students. Their value can also be found in their portrayal of student survival. They are valuable for what they tell us about the past. I hope they will also inspire modern Haskell students and Native peoples in general.

As stated in the beginning, I set out on this journey looking for stories that were waiting to be discovered, waiting to be told. It was a rocky path much of the way, and sometimes I could not see around a bend and sometimes I had to climb over some pretty big boulders. But there was beautiful scenery along the way, and as I come to the end of this path of historical inquiry, I can say with a light heart—at least some of the 19th century Haskell students' stories of sacrifice and survival have now been told.

REFERENCES AND WORKS CITED

References

[1] Anderson, 1997; Hoffman, 1964;Vuckovic, 2001.

[2] Adams, 1995; Anderson, 1997;Vuckovic, 2001.

[3] Anderson, 1997;Vuckovic, 2001.

[4] Anderson, 1997;Vuckovic, 2001; et al. See photograph 1.

[5] *Annual Report to the Commissioner of Indian Affairs*, 1885; Anderson, 1997; Goddard, 1930.

[6] *Annual Report to the Commissioner of Indian Affairs*, 1887; Anderson, 1997; Goddard, 1930.

[7] Anderson, 1997; Goddard, 1930;Vuckovic, 2001.

[8] Anderson, 1997.

[9] *Annual Reports of the Commissioner of Indian Affairs*, 1894–1897; Goddard, 1930.

[10] Goddard, 1930;Vuckovic, 2001.

[11] Grabowski, *Annual Report to the Commissioner of Indian Affairs*, 1886; Swett, *Annual Report to the Commissioner of Indian Affairs*, 1895, p. 374.

[12] Swett, *Annual Report to the Commissioner of Indian Affairs*, 1896, p. 375.

[13] Correspondence from the Office of Indian Affairs, National Archives, September 1902;Vuckovic, 2001; Haskell Athletics 1884–2004, 120th anniversary program.

[14] *Annual Reports to the Commissioner of Indian Affairs*, 1884, 1887, 1891, 1901.

[15] *Haskell Registration Ledger, 1884–1889*, p. 84–87; p. 212–215.

[16] *Haskell Registration Ledger, 1884–1889*, p. 18–21.

[17] Ames, 1936, p. 2; Granzer, 1937, p. 24.

[18] Anderson, 1997, p. 24;Vuckovic, 2001, p. 46; *Haskell Registration Ledger, 1884–1889*.

[19] Goddard, 1930; Granzer, 1937; Hoffman, 1964; Anderson, 1997;Vuckovic, 2001.

[20] Adams, 1995.

[21] Charles and Sara T.D. Robinson Collection, 1834–1911, Kansas State Historical Society.

[22] Charles and Sara T.D. Robinson Collection, 1834–1911, Kansas State Historical Society; *Haskell Registration Ledger, 1884–1889*, p. 248–251; student files.

[23] Charles and Sara T.D. Robinson Collection, 1834–1911, Kansas State Historical Society; *Haskell Registration Ledger, 1884–1889*, p. 338–341.

[24] *Annual Reports to the Commissioner of Indian Affairs*, 1886–1894.

[25] Charles and Sara T.D. Robinson Collection, 1834–1911, Kansas State Historical Society; *Haskell Registration Ledger, 1884–1889*; Haskell Cemetery.

[26] Student Files, National Archives, KCMO.

27 *Haskell Registration Ledger, 1884–1889*, p. 268–271; Haskell Cemetery.

28 Charles and Sara T.D. Robinson Collection, 1834–1911.

29 *Annual Reports to the Commissioner of Indian Affairs*, 1886–1894.

30 *Haskell Registration Ledger, 1884–1889*, p. 268–271.

31 Child, 1998, p. 55; Adams, 1995; Anderson, 1997; Vuckovic, 2001; Child, 1998, p. 56.

32 Copy of actual letter is included with photos later in text.

33 Charles and Sara T.D. Robinson Collection, 1834–1911.

34 Ibid.

35 Ibid.

36 Ibid.

37 Ibid.; *Haskell Registration Ledger, 1884–1889*, p. 216–224.

38 *Haskell Registration Ledger, 1884–1889*, p. 216–224.

39 Adams, 1995; Child, 1998; Lomawaima, 1994; Trennert, 1988; Anderson, 1997; Vuckovic, 2001.

40 *Haskell Registration Ledger, 1884*–1889; Haskell Cemetery tombstones; Student files.

41 Charles and Sara T.D. Robinson Collection, 1834–1911; *Haskell Registration Ledger, 1884–1889*, p. 284–287; 220–223; Student files, National Archives, KCMO; Haskell Cemetery.

42 Anderson, 1996, p. 132.

43 Grabowski, *Annual Report to the Commissioner of Indian Affairs*, 1886, p. 6.

44 Robinson, *Annual Report to the Commissioner of Indian Affairs*, 1887, p. 238.

45 Anderson, 1997; Vuckovic, 2001.

46 *The Indian Leader*, September 28, 1900, Vol. IV, no. 26, p. 2.

47 *The Indian Leader*, 1918, p. 2.

48 Anderson, 1997, p. 50–51; ibid, p. 82; Ibid., p. 161.

49 Little, 1980, p. 136.

50 Correspondence from Commissioner of Indian Affairs and Student Files, National Archives, KCMO; *The Indian Leader*, Vol. I, No. 11, p. 3.

51 *The Indian Leader*, Vol. II, No. 1, p. 3.

52 *The Indian Leader*, Vol. II, No. 9, p. 2.

53 *The Indian Leader*, July 1898, Vol. II, No. 5, p. 3.

54 *The Indian Leader*, October 1898, Vol. II, No. 10, p. 3; March 1899, Vol. III, No. 1, p. 2.

55 *The Indian Leader*, April 1899, Vol. III, No. 2, p. 4.

56 *The Indian Leader*, August 1899, Vol. III, No. 16, p. 3; October 1899, Vol. III, No. 17, p. 3.

57 *The Indian Leader*, November 1899, Vol. III, No. 20, p. 3.

58 Grabowski, *Annual Report to the Commissioner of Indian Affairs*, 1886, p. 6.

59 Student Files, National Archives, KCMO.

60 *The Indian Leader*, Vol. V, No. 24, p. 2.

61 *The Indian Leader*, June 1919, Vol. XXII, No. 40, p. 15–16.

[62] *The Indian Leader,* January, 1909, Vol. XIII, No. 4, p. 5.

[63] Grabowski, *Annual Report to the Commissioner of Indian Affairs,* 1886, p. 6.

[64] Charles and Sara T.D. Robinson Collection, 1834–1911.

[65] Ibid.

[66] *Haskell Registration Ledger, 1884–1889,* p. 156–159, 244–247.

[67] *Haskell Registration Ledger, 1884–1889,* p. 132–135; Charles and Sara T.D. Robinson Collection, 1834–1911; *The Indian Leader,* June 1919, Alumni Issue, p. 13.

[68] Anderson, 1997, p. 161.

[69] *Haskell Registration Ledger, 1884–1889,* p. 244–247.

[70] Charles and Sara T.D. Robinson Collection, 1834–1911.

[71] *Haskell Registration Ledger, 1884–1889; The Indian Leader.*

[72] *The Indian Leader,* June 1919, p. 15–16; 22; 29, 20–21.

[73] *The Indian Leader,* June 1919, p. 21.

[74] *The Indian Leader,* January 12, 1900, Vol. III, no. 27, p. 3.

[75] *The Indian Leader,* January 19, 1900, Vol. III, no. 28, p. 3.

[76] *The Indian Leader,* March 2, 1900, Vol. III, no. 34, p. 2.

[77] *The Indian Leader,* March 9, 1900, Vol. III, no. 35, p. 3.

[78] *The Indian Leader,* April 20, 1900, Vol. IV, no. 7, p. 2.

[79] *Annual Reports of the Commissioner of Indian Affairs;* Anderson, 1997; Vuckovic, 2001; *The Indian Leader.*

[80] Dorchester, *Annual Report to the Commissioner of Indian Affairs,* 1889, p. 322; Swett, *Annual Report to the Commissioner of Indian Affairs,* 1894, p. 382.

[81] Swett, *Annual Report to the Commissioner of Indian Affairs,* 1895, p. 374.

[82] Swett, *Annual Report to the Commissioner of Indian Affairs,* 1896, p. 376.

[83] Swett, *Annual Report to the Commissioner of Indian Affairs,* 1897, p. 351.

[84] Horowitz, 1987, p. 29; Wetzel, 1950, p. 430; Little, 1980, p. 137.

[85] *The Indian Leader,* October 1897, Vol. I, no. 9, p. 3.

[86] *The Indian Leader,* March 1898, Vol. II, no. 1, p. 2.

[87] *The Indian Leader,* August 1897, Vol. I, no. 7, p. 2.

[88] *The Indian Leader,* Vol. II, no. 11, p. 2.

[89] Swett, *Annual Report to the Commissioner of Indian Affairs,* 1895, p. 373; 1896, p. 375–376.

[90] Swett, *Annual Report to the Commissioner of Indian Affairs,* 1895, p. 374.

[91] Hailmann, 1899, p. 18.

[92] Swett, *Annual Report to the Commissioner of Indian Affairs,* 1896, p. 375.

[93] Swett, *Annual Report to the Commissioner of Indian Affairs,* 1897, p. 351.

[94] Ibid

[95] Pratt, *Annual Report to the Commissioner of Indian Affairs,* 1897, p. 373.

[96] Ogren, 2005, p. 4.

[97] Ibid., p. 86

[98] Hailmann, 1899, p. 20.

[99] Ogren, 2005, p. 4–5.

[100] Ibid., p. 19.

[101] *The Indian Leader*, June 1897, Vol. I, no. 5, p. 1; p. 2.

[102] *The Indian Leader*, June 1897, Vol. I, no. 5, p. 1; p. 3; p. 7.

[103] *The Indian Leader*, June 1897, Vol. I, no. 5, p. 6; p. 7.

[104] Ogren, 2005, p. 100.

[105] Ibid., p. 108.

[106] Swett, *Annual Report to the Commissioner of Indian Affairs*, 1894, p. 382.

[107] *The Indian Leader*, March, 1897, Vol. I, no. 1, p. 3.

[108] *The Indian Leader*, Vol. II, no. 10, p. 3.

[109] Ogren, 2005, p. 162.

[110] *The Indian Leader*, June 1897, Vol. I, no. 5, p. 4.

[111] *The Indian Leader*, June 1897, Vol. I, no. 5, p. 3.

[112] *The Indian Leader*, April 1897, Vol. I, no. 2, p. 2.

[113] *The Indian Leader*, April 1897, Vol. I, no. 2, p. 2.

[114] *The Indian Leader*, May 1897, Vol. I, no. 3, p. 2.

[115] *The Indian Leader*, Vol. I, no. 10, p. 2.

[116] *The Indian Leader*, Vol. I, no. 13, p. 2.

[117] *The Indian Leader*, Vol. II, no. 2, p. 2.

[118] *The Indian Leader*, May 11, 1900, Vol. IV, no. 10, p. 3.

[119] Anderson, 1997; Taft, 1955.

[120] *The Indian Leader*, April, 1897, Vol. I, no. 2, p. 3.

[121] *The Indian Leader*, Vol. I, no. 3, p. 3.

[122] *The Indian Leader*, Vol. I, no. 4, June 1897, p. 3.

[123] Hailmann, 1899, p. 21.

[124] *The Indian Leader*, May 1897, Vol. I, no. 3, p. 2.

[125] Sterling, 1891; *The Cicala*, 1884, p. 80.

[126] *The Cicala*, 1884, p. 81, p. 7–8.

[127] Vuckovic, 2001, p. 173.

[128] Horowitz, 1987, p. 4.

Works Cited

Primary Sources

Archival Collections

Haskell Registration Ledger, 1884–1889, Haskell Cultural Center and Museum, Haskell Indian Nations University, Lawrence, KS

Charles and Sara T.D. Robinson Collection, 1834–1911, Kansas State Historical Society, Topeka, KS

Kenneth Spencer Research Library, University of Kansas, Lawrence, KS

Student Files, National Archives, Central Plains Region, Kansas City, MO. Records of the Bureau of Indian Affairs, Record Group 75.

Government Documents

United States Department of the Interior, Office of Indian Affairs. *Annual Reports of the Commissioner of Indian Affairs to the Secretary of the Interior.* Washington: Government Printing Office, 1886–1889, 1892–1899, 1901–1903.

Newspapers & Annuals

The Cicala. University Press of Kansas, Lawrence, KS, 1884.

The Indian Leader. Haskell Institute, Lawrence, KS, 1897–1900.

Lawrence Daily Journal. Lawrence, KS, 1894, 1895, 1897.

Autobiographies

Birch, C.E. (1949). *John Faithful: Schoolmaster.* New York: The Exposition Press.

Horne, E.B. and McBeth, S. (1998). *Essie's Story: The Life and Legacy of a Shoshone Teacher.* Lincoln: University of Nebraska Press.

Standing Bear, L. (1975). *My People The Sioux.* Lincoln: University of Nebraska Press.

Winnie, L. (1969). *Sah-Gan-De-Oh: The Chief's Daughter.* New York: Vantage Press.

Zitkala-Sa, G.B.S. (1902). *An Indian Teacher Among Indians.* New York: Atlantic Monthly.

Secondary Sources

Adams, D.W. (1995). *Education for Extinction: American Indians and the Boarding School Experience, 1875–1928.* Lawrence, KS: University Press of Kansas.

Adams, E.C. (1971). *American Indian Education: Government Schools and Economic Progress.* (American Education: its men, ideas, and institutions. Series II). New York: Arno Press and The New York Times.

Ahern, W.H. (1997, Spring). An Experiment Aborted: Returned Indian Students in the Indian School Service, 1881–1908. *Ethnohistory*, 44(2), 263–304.

Altom, M. C. (2000) *Students at Haskell Institute from 1884 to 1889*. Lawrence, KS: Haskell Cultural Center and Museum.

Anderson, E. P. (1997). *An Imperfect Education: Assimilation and American Indians at Haskell Institute, Lawrence, Kansas, 1884–1894*. Thesis: University of Kansas, Lawrence, KS.

Archuleta, M.L., Child, B. J. and Lomawaima, K. T. (Eds.). (2000) *Away from Home: American Indian Boarding School Experiences, 1879–2000*. Phoenix, AZ: The Heard Museum.

Carter, P. (1995). Completely Discouraged: Women Teachers' Resistance in the Bureau of Indian Affairs Schools, 1900–1910. *Frontiers*, 15(3), 53–86.

Child, B.J. (1998). *Boarding School Seasons: American Indian Families, 1900–1940*. Lincoln: University of Nebraska Press.

Coleman, M.C. (1993). *American Indian Children at School, 1850–1930*. Jackson: University Press of Mississippi.

Edmumds, R.D. (1995, June). Native Americans, New Voices: American Indian History, 1895–1995. *The American Historical Review*, 100(3), 717–740.

Fischbacher, T. (1967). *A Study of the Role of the Federal Government in the Education of the American Indian*. Dissertation: Arizona State University.

Goddard, G. (1930). *A Study of the Historical Development and Educational Work at Haskell Institute*. Thesis: Kansas State Teacher's College, Emporia, KS.

Granzer, M.L. (1937). *Education at Haskell Institute, 1884–1937*. Thesis: University of Nebraska.

Hale, L. (2002). *Native American Education: A Reference Handbook*. (Contemporary Education Issues). Denver: ABC CLIO, Inc.

Hailmann, W.N. (1899). Education of the Indian. *Monographs on Education in the United States*. Ed. Nicholas Murray Butler. New York: J.B. Lyon Company.

Hatfield, W.W. (Jun., 1926). General and Specialized Literary Clubs. *The English Journal*. 15(6), 450–456.

Hewes, D.W. (1981). Those First Good Years of Indian Education: 1894–1898. *American Indian Culture and Research Journal*, 5(2), 63–82.

Hoffman, R. (1964). *A History of the Commercial Department of Haskell Institute, 1895–1963*. Thesis: Pittsburg State University, Pittsburg, KS.

Hoxie, F.E. (1984). *A Final Promise: The Campaign to Assimilate the Indians, 1880–1920*. New York: Cambridge University Press.

Hyer, S. (1990). *One House, One Voice, One Heart: Native American Education at the Santa Fe Indian School*. Santa Fe: Museum of New Mexico Press.

Johnson, D.L. and Wilson, R. (1988, Winter). Gertrude Simmons Bonnin, 1876–1938: "Americanize the First American". *American Indian Quarterly*, 12(1), 27–40.

Landis, B. (1996). *Carlisle Indian Industrial School History* [electronic version]. Retrieved September 9, 2005 from http://home.epix.net/~landis/histry.html

Lee, A. (Jan., 1924). Literary Societies in a Small High School. *The English Journal.* 13(1), p. 35–38.

Lomawaima, K.T. (1993, May). Domesticity in the Federal Indian Schools: The Power of Authority over Mind and Body. *American Ethnologist,* 20(2), 227–240.

Lomawaima, K.T. (1994). *They Called It Prairie Light: The Story of Chilocco Indian School.* Lincoln: University of Nebraska Press.

Lomawaima, K.T. (1996, Spring). Estelle Reel, Superintendent of Indian Schools: 1898–1910: Politics, Curriculum, and Land. *Journal of American Indian Education,* 35(3), 5–31.

Mihesuah, D.A. (1993). *Cultivating the Rosebuds: The Education of Women at the Cherokee Female Seminary, 1851–1909.* Champaign: University of Illinois Press.

Ogren, C.A. (2005). *The American State Normal School: "An Instrument of Great Good."* New York: Palgrave Macmillan.

Pratt, R.H. (1964). *Battlefield and Classroom: Four Decades with the American Indian, 1867–1904.* New Haven: Yale University Press.

Prucha, F.P. (1979). *The Churches and the Indian Schools, 1888–1912.* Lincoln: University of Nebraska Press.

Reyhner, J.A. and Eder, J. (2004). *American Indian Education: A History.* Norman: University of Oklahoma Press.

Riney, S.D. (1999). *The Rapid City Indian School, 1898–1933.* Norman: University of Oklahoma Press.

Robinson, M.K. (1996). *Assimilation, Ambivalence, and Resistance: Students at Haskell Institute, 1920–1930.* Thesis: University of Kansas, Lawrence, KS.

Sterling, W. (Ed.) (1891). *Quarter-Centennial History of the University of Kansas, 1866–1891.* Topeka: Geo. W. Crane & Co.

Taft, R. (1955). *The Years on Mount Oread.* Lawrence: University of Kansas Press.

Trennert, R.A. (1982, July). Educating Indian Girls at Nonreservation Boarding Schools, 1878–1920. *The Western Historical Quarterly,* 13(3), 271–290.

Trennert, R.A. (1988). *The Phoenix Indian School: Forced Assimilation in Arizona, 1891–1935.* Norman: University of Oklahoma Press.

Vuckovic, M. (2001). *"Onward Ever, Backward Never:" Student Life and Students' Lives at Haskell Institute, 1884–1920s.* Dissertation: University of Kansas, Lawrence, KS.

Wetzel, A. (May, 1905). Student Organizations in a High School. *The School Review,* 13(5), 429–433.

Witmer, L.F. (1993). *The Indian Industrial School: Carlisle, Pennsylvania, 1879–1918.* Huggins Printing Company, Harrisburg, PA.

Haskell Cemetery Walking Tour

On the southeastern side of the main Haskell campus is an area with trees standing at each corner of the short chain-link fence surrounding rows of tombstones. Most of the tombstones were ordered and placed in the cemetery in the 1930s. This guide begins at the northeast corner.

The following information in the first three lines is taken directly from the tombstones in the cemetery.

The details or obituaries that follow, if any, have been gathered from one of three sources. The earliest are taken from the 1884–1889 Haskell Student Registration List, which has different spelling or names or ages. Additionally, in a few cases, there was reference made in letters found in the Charles and Sara T.D. Robinson Collection. After 1897, many of the deaths were memorialized in *The Indian Leader.*

FIRST ROW, NORTHEAST CORNER

Cora La Fromboise
Potawatomi
1872–1885

Cora LaFromboise, Potawatomi, arrived from Maple Hill, Kansas, on September 8, 1885 at the age of 13. Her parent/guardian is listed as J. Smith, Maple Hill, Kansas. She died on November 6, 1885.

(1884–1889 Registration List)

Frank Clark
Potawatomi
1868–1885

Frank Clark, half Potawatomi, was 16 years old when he arrived from Silver Lake, KS on November 13, 1884. His parent/guardian was Angeline Radigem from Silver Lake. Frank died on November 11, 1885.

(1884–1889 Registration List)

Norman Brockey
Pawnee
1861–1885

Norman Brockey, a full Pawnee who was once known as *Kee-wa koo-tah-ra ñoose,* arrived on September 19, 1884, from Pawnee, Indian Territory. He was 20 years old at the time; there is no parent/guardian listed. He died on January 12, 1885.

(1884–1889 Registration List)

Charles Panther
Osage
1865–1885

At 20 years of age, Osage **Charles Panther** arrived at Haskell on January 25, 1885. He died less than a month later on February 14, 1885.

(1884–1889 Registration List)

Stephen Kimball
Ponca
1868–1885

Steve Kimbal, or *Deh-de-tha*, arrived on November 13, 1884, at the age of 16. A full Ponca, he was the son of Dick Kimbal from Ponca, Indian Territory. He died on May 19, 1885.

(1884–1889 Registration List)

Chester Lone Walk
Pawnee
1869–1885

Chester Lone Walk, full Pawnee, was 15 years old when he arrived on September 19, 1884 from Pawnee, Indian Territory. Once known as *La-tah-kuta-ta-kah*, the young man died on April 2, 1885.

(1884–1889 Registration List)

Thomas Tuttle
Osage
1866–1885

Thomas Tuttle was a 19-year-old Osage who arrived on January 1, 1885. He died ten days later, on January 11, 1885.

(1884–1889 Registration List)

Harry White Wolf
Cheyenne
Died 1884 Aged 6 mos

On September 19, 1884, two days after the official opening ceremony, a wagon arrived at Haskell with forty-two Cheyenne and Arapahoe children and parents. Among the group were multiple family
units, including White Wolf and his wife Mrs. White Wolf, daughter,
Grover White Wolf, and infant son, Harry White Wolf. The drastically
changing weather and inadequate heating in the uncompleted buildings resulted in a number of deaths during the school's first six months.
Harry White Wolf, Cheyenne, was the first fatality.

(1884–1889 Registration List)

Willie Erye
Pawnee
1871–1885

Willie Ayre, a full Pawnee once known as *Te-eet*, arrived from Pawnee, Indian Territory, on September 1, 1884, at the age of 13. He died
on February 26, 1885.

(1884–1889 Registration List)

Lizzie King
Peoria
1868–1885

Lizzie King, a 16-year-old Peoria, arrived on December 15, 1884.
She died on April 17, 1885.

(1884–1889 Registration List)

Seth Thomas
Osage
1867–1885

At 17 years of age, Osage **Seth Thomas** arrived at Haskell on December 15, 1884. He was here two months and died on February 16, 1885.

(1884–1889 Registration List)

Andrew Williams
Pawnee
1867–1885

Andrew Williams, a full Pawnee from Pawnee, Indian Territory, was 17 years old when he arrived on September 19, 1884. He died on March 17, 1885.

(1884–1889 Registration List)

Herbert Scheshewalla
Osage
1866–1886

Herbert Scheshewalla was 19 years of age when he arrived on October 29, 1885. He was full Osage; his parent/guardian is listed as *Strike Ax*. Herbert died on December 31, 1886.

(1884–1889 Registration List)

Lena Cage
Pawnee
1881–1887

Once known as *Stah-kah*, **Lena Cage** was a 6-year-old Pawnee who arrived on March 5, 1887. Her parent/guardian was *Le-te-tes-te* from Pawnee Agency, Indian Territory. Lena died the same month she arrived, March 1887; the actual day was not recorded.

(1884–1889 Registration List)

Clarence White
Pawnee
1874–1887

Clarence White, a full Pawnee whose Native name translated as
White Wolf, was 13 years old when he arrived on March 5, 1887. His
parent/guardian was *Teh-rah-wah-battorahny* from Pawnee, Indian Territory. Clarence died August 13, 1887; the cause of death is listed as
consumption (tuberculosis).

(1884–1889 Registration List)

Eberhald Howell
Pawnee
1873–1887

Once known as *Lih-sah-list-i-tats-ah*, **Eberhald Howell**, a 14-year-old
full Pawnee, arrived at Haskell with his brother George on December 15, 1886. His parent/guardian was Joseph Howell from Pawnee
Agency. He died on March 7, 1887.

(1884–1889 Registration List)

Charley Reynolds
Arapahoe
1871–1888

Charley Reynolds, a full Arapahoe from Darlington, Indian Territory,
arrived on July 1, 1885 at the age of 14. He died on January 5, 1888,
of pneumonia.

(1884–1889 Registration List)

Peter Siler
Mojave
1863–1887

At 22 years of age, **Peter Siler**, full Mojave, arrived from Ft. Grant, Indian Territory. On July 1, 1885. He died of consumption on June 24, 1887.

(1884–1889 Registration List)

Somebody's Son
Unknown
Unknown

Somebody's Daughter
Unknown
Unknown

Maggie Big Fire
Cheyenne
1869–1887

Maggie Big Fire, or *Mahyoun Ahgi,* was 15 when she arrived in September 1884. A full Cheyenne, she was the daughter of *Big Fire* from Darlington, Indian Territory. Maggie died on August 19, 1887 due to consumption.

(1884–1889 Registration List)

Bird McGuire
Osage
1869–1887

Once known as *Wah-sir-tah,* **Bird McGuire** was a 16-year-old full Osage who arrived at Haskell on December 16, 1885. His parent/guardian is listed as *Homihah kah* from Osage Agency. Bird died on November 5, 1887.

(1884–1889 Registration List)

May Mohajah
Kaw
1880–1887

May Mohajah was 7 when she arrived at Haskell from the Kaw Agency on July 1, 1887, with her sister Ada Mohajah, who was 10. May did not make it through the winter. She passed away on December 18, 1887. Her parent/guardian is listed as John Mohajah from Kaw Agency.

(1884–1889 Registration List)

Somebody's Grandson
Unknown
Unknown

Somebody's Granddaughter
Unknown
Unknown

Adam Swamp
Oneida
1878–1892

Josiah Patterson
Pawnee
1868–1893

Josiah Patterson, or *Ah-cah-she*, was a 16-year-old, full Pawnee who arrived on September 19, 1884. He was from Pawnee, Indian Territory; his parent/guardian was *Ta-pa-koo-no-ke-wah-ah-too*. His first four-year term expired on July 2, 1888, and he left the institution for two months. Josiah "re-entered for two years Aug. 22, 1888."

(1884–1889 Registration List)

Ada Mohajah
Kaw
1878–1893

Ada Mohajah, a Kaw who was 10 years of age when she arrived at Haskell with her little sister, May, on July 1, 1887, continued at Haskell for the next five years. There is no indication she went home to her parent/guardian John Mohajah at the Kaw Agency over the five years following her sister May's death. Ada died on January 21, 1893.

(1884–1889 Registration List; Student Files)

Carrie Pendleton
Cheyenne
1879–1893

Jack LaForce
Osage
1880–1894

Jack LaForce, a 7-year-old Osage from Osage Agency, arrived at Haskell on April 18, 1888. His parent/guardian was Peter LaForce.

(1884–1889 Registration List)

Nelson Vitolia
Papago
1883–1901

SECOND ROW, SOUTH TO NORTH

Arleigh Perry
Chippewa
1882–1901

The following obituary was printed in the January 4, 1901 issue of *The Indian Leader:*

Arleigh Perry

On Saturday afternoon, December 29, the earthly life of **Arleigh Perry** ended. He had been sick only two weeks, but the disease, pneumonia, had such a strong hold that medical skill and careful nursing could not save the young life. Arleigh was not yet twenty, a bright, pleasant boy well-liked by his teachers and school mates. When told that he could not live he said of course he would like to get well, but was not afraid to die; he could trust Jesus to take care of him.

Arleigh's mother did not reach here until after his death but his little sister was with him and was as devoted and faithful as the mother could have been.

The funeral was held on Sunday afternoon at three o'clock. Dr. Dixon's sermon was earnest and impressive and the music most appropriate. The flowers were beautiful. They were offerings from his teacher, Sunday school teacher, classmates and other friends.   (p. 2)

Charles Adams
Pawnee
1884–1900

The following obituary was printed in the May 4, 1900, issue of *The Indian Leader:*

Charlie Adams, a Pawnee, aged about fifteen years, died at six o'clock a.m. Sunday, April 20. He was a quiet, delicate, gentlemanly boy who had many friends among his associates. During his short illness he was patient and cheerful. When asked how he felt he always said with a smile "Better." Charlie's father came two weeks before his death and was constantly by his bedside, showing touching love and devotion. Charlie's last word was "Father," in his native tongue, then with a bright smile he "passed away." Mr. Adams said he felt sure his son was with the Great Spirit because his face wore such a peaceful, happy expression. Late Sunday afternoon the funeral service was held in the chapel. The pallbearers were officers from the companies in the small boys' building where Charlie had roomed. The neat coffin was covered with beautiful roses, lilies and other flowers brought by employes and pupils. Dr. Dixon conducted the service, which was touching and impressive. The remains were followed to the little cemetery by almost the whole school.   (p. 3)

Charlie Edge
Caddo
1879–1900

Charles Edge was in the 2nd grade according to the February 1, 1899 issue of *The Indian Leader*. In the March 2, 1900 issue the following item is printed under "Shoe Shop Items":

We are sorry to say that **Charles Edge** is now on the sick list. But we hope to have him with us again soon.   (p. 2)

The March 23, 1900 issue includes two items:

The devotion of Sam and Willie Weller to **Charles Edge** during his illness was beautiful. They were with him day and night and by their intelligent helpfulness were of great assistance to Mrs. Seeley.

The following obituary was printed in the March 23, 1900 issue of *The Indian Leader*.

Charles Edge
Charles Edge, a Caddo, aged about eighteen, died last Wednesday morning after a short illness. He had not been really well for some time, but said nothing about how he felt until so ill that he was compelled to give up and go to the hospital; then the disease had such a hold upon him that medical skill and careful nursing were of no avail. Charles spoke English imperfectly, so talked but little except when with his Caddo friends, but he always had a pleasant smile and greeting for all whom he met. One of his teachers said of him, "He was such a dear boy; so good natured and pleasant; so obedient and willing." Charles' parents who live near Anadarko, Oklahoma, have the sympathy of the friends here.

The impressive funeral service was conducted by Rev. G. D. Rogers, of the Lawrence Baptist Church, at 9:30 A.M. on Thursday. There were many beautiful flowers, the offerings of his teacher and other friends.

(p. 3)

Johnson Peabody
Omaha
1892–1901

According to the September 15, 1898 issue of *The Indian Leader,* **Johnson Peabody** arrived with his brother Walter in September, 1898. The following item was printed in the May 1, 1899 issue of *The Indian Leader:*

"Little **Johnson Peabody** looked unhappy the other day and when asked 'What is the matter, Johnson?' replied 'measle-sick.'"   (p. 3)

Another item was included in the June 15, 1899 issue:

Johnson Peabody was proudly displaying a new fish line the other morning and was soon after seen fishing very industriously over the railing of the back porch. There was no water below but that was a small matter.   (p. 3)

The April 13, 1900 issue included this item in the section on "The Kindergarten":

The small boys in the Kindergarten were very enthusiastic over base ball last Wednesday morning. A nine has been organized consisting of the little ones. The names and positions of those on the team were not learned but Erwin Spooner announced clearly that he was a substitute. Leo Burnett wore the colors—which were very like those worn by the foot-ball team last fall—and **Johnson Peabody** had on a glove. In the same issue Johnson is listed as a pupil in the Kindergarten class.

The following obituary was printed in the January 11, 1901 issue of *The Indian Leader:*

Little **Johnson Peabody**, who has been suffering from tuberculosis for some time, died last Saturday night. When Johnson came here a year and a half ago he could not talk English but learned the language very readily and was much in earnest about his school work. His teacher always spoke of him as "such a dear boy." The funeral service was conducted by Rev. Bamford, of Lawrence, on Sunday afternoon. Beautiful flowers were laid about the little face and on the coffin by his teacher and Sunday school teacher.   (p. 2–3)

Mary Pahmahine
Potawatomi
1893–1900

The following obituary was printed in the August 31, 1900 issue of *The Indian Leader:*

"Little Mary is dead," was the sad news which was told at breakfast last Monday morning. **Mary Pahmahmie** was one of our smallest girls and was a general favorite on account of her bright smiles and gentle, winning ways. She was not sick long but suffered greatly. The end came at 6:15 A.M. Monday. Her father came Tuesday morning and the little body was taken home to Jackson county, Kansas, for burial.   (p. 3)

George C. Evans
Shawnee
1882–1894

Peter Pearson
Pawnee
1876–1889

Peter Pearson, a 13-year-old Pawnee from Pawnee, Indian Territory, arrived at Haskell on April 1, 1888. He died of consumption on May 10, 1889.

(1884–1889 Registration List)

Joseph Blackburn
Pawnee
1879–1889

Joseph Blackburn, a full Pawnee, was eight years old when he arrived on September 15, 1887, from Pawnee, Indian Territory.

In April 1888, the superintendent was notified:

> Haskell   Apr. 4th, 1888
> Gov. Robinson,
>   I am sorry to say that Joe Blackburn is down with a severe type of typhoid pneumonia, coming in on Monday(?), but developed nothing serious till yesterday. He seems to promise a very bad case.
>   Very Respectfully Yours, V. W. May

Joseph died of consumption on February 16, 1889.

(1884–1889 Registration List; Charles Robinson Collection)

Mary Riley
Seminole
1871–1888

It appears that **Mary Riley**, a 17-year-old Seminole, arrived at Haskell on August 27, 1888. She died on October 7, 1888.

(1884–1889 Registration List)

Martha Campbell
Seminole
1870–1888

Martha Campbell, an 18-year-old Seminole, arrived on the same day as Mary Riley, August 27, 1888. Martha also died on the same day, October 7, 1888.

(1884–1889 Registration List)

Perry Little Elk
Cheyenne
1875–1888

Perry Little Elk, or *Hoohah*, was 9-years-old when he arrived at Haskell from Darlington, Indian Territory on September 19, 1884 with his parents, Tommie and Mrs. Little Elk and his little sister Laura, who was 3. A full Cheyenne, Perry died of pneumonia on October 2, 1888.

(1884–1889 Registration List)

Samuel Vallier
Quapaw
1877–1888

Samuel Valier was a 10-year-old Quapaw from Baxter Springs who arrived on September 1, 1887. He died of pneumonia on May 22, 1888.

(1884–1889 Registration List)

Willie Sears
Sioux
1872–1888

Willie Sears, a 15-year-old Sioux, arrived at Haskell with his 10-year-old brother, Vincent, on September 15, 1887 from Kaw Agency, Indian Territory. His parent/guardian was Mr. Sears. Willie died on May 18, 1888—the cause of death listed—"Accidentally Killed."

(1884–1889 Registration List)

Chester Big Tree
Winnebago
1873–1888

Chester Big Tree, Winnebago, was 14 years of age when he arrived on July 1, 1887; his parent was Big Tree. Chester died on May 15, 1888; the cause was pneumonia.

(1884–1889 Registration List)

Jessie D. Murie
Pawnee
1873–1888

Jessie Murie, or *Tah-kah,* was a 14-year-old full Pawnee who arrived on March 5, 1887; Charlie Murie from Pawnee, Indian Territory, was his parent/guardian. Jessie died from pneumonia on May 9, 1888.

(1884–1889 Registration List)

Andrew Big Snake
Ponca
1872–1888

A Ponca, **Andrew Big Snake,** was 15 years of age when he arrived on August 19, 1887; his parent/guardian was John DeLodge from Ponca, Indian Territory. Andrew died on May 6, 1888, of pneumonia.

(1884–1889 Registration List)

James Beaver
Wiandotte
1876–1888

James Beaver, an 11-year-old Wyandotte from Baxter Springs, arrived at Haskell on September 1, 1887. He died of pneumonia on May 2, 1888.

(1884–1889 Registration List)

Edna Eaves
Pawnee
1877–1888

Edna Eaves, once known as *Asshtorse*, was a 10-year-old Pawnee who arrived on March 5, 1887; her parent/guardian was *Lasahcoralehorasale* from Pawnee, Indian Territory. Edna died on April 18, 1888.

(1884–1889 Registration List)

Fred Sumner
Kaw
1877–1888

Fred Sumner was a full Kaw who arrived on October 22, 1884 at the age of 7 from Kaw Agency. He died on April 17, 1888.

(1884–1889 Registration List)

Guy Meachem
Pawnee
1880–1888

Guy Meachem, a full Pawnee, arrived at Haskell on March 5, 1887. Once known as *Gah-me-tah*, his parent/guardian was *Seven Stars* from Pawnee, Indian Territory. Guy died of pneumonia on April 17, 1888.

(1884–1889 Registration List)

Metopo Cheauteau
Osage
1872–1888

Metofo Cheauteau was a 14-year-old Osage female who arrived on July 13, 1886. Her parent/guardian was Gus Choteau from Osage Agency, Indian Territory.

On April 2, 1888, Haskell Superintendent Robinson received the following note from the school's hospital:

Hospital April 2nd 1888

Gov. Robinson

I have to report that Metofa Choteau is in a critical condition. She is one of those bad constitutional cases that took pneumonia early last month, having previously had longstanding discharging ulcers on the legs. But recently healed; she appeared to improve in the lung trouble till lately, the cough remaining solid, and a tubucular, ? diarrhea is now running her down. The liver is also seriously affected. It is exceeding probable, considering her history, that the case will soon prove fatal.

Respectfully Yours, V.W. May

Metofo died on April 3, 1888.

(1884–1889 Registration List; Charles Robinson Collection)

Willie Gibson
Caddo
1877–1888

Willie Gibson, or *Lance-as-English*, a 10-year-old Caddo, arrived on April 2, 1887. His parent/guardian was John Gibson from Anadarko, Indian Territory. Willie died on March 10, 1888 from pneumonia.

(1884–1889 Registration List)

John Guy
Caddo
1877–1888

John Guy, a full Caddo once known as *Te-wy-nors*, was 10 years old when he arrived on April 2, 1887. His parent/guardian was *Poncha* from Anadarko, Indian Territory. He died on February 13, 1888.

(1884–1889 Registration List)

Somebody's Sister
Unknown
Unknown

Somebody's Brother
Unknown
Unknown

Fred Yellow Eyes
Cheyenne
1874–1886

Fred Yellow Eyes, or Yellow Louse, was a full Cheyenne who arrived on November 12, 1885 at the age of 11. His parent/guardian was Yellow Eyes from Darlington, Indian Territory. Fred died on April 2, 1886.

(1884–1889 Registration List)

James Buell
Cheyenne
1869–1886

James Buell arrived on July 1, 1885. He died on April 2, 1886
(1884–1889 Registration List)

Agnes McCarty
Modoc
1870–1886

Agnes McCarty was a 14-year-old Modoc who arrived on September 15, 1884, from Baxter Springs. She died in May ,1886.

(1884–1889 Registration List)

Nellie Hand
Arapahoe
1871–1886

A 13-year-old Arapahoe, **Lillie Hand**, arrived from Darlington, Indian Territory, in September 1884. She died on January 13, 1886.

(1884–1889 Registration List)

Eugene Barber
Cheyenne
1877–1885

Eugene Barber, Cheyenne, arrived on December 15, 1884. He died on November 13, 1885.

(1884–1889 Registration List)

THIRD ROW, NORTH TO SOUTH

Moses Holmes
Ponca
1871–1886

Moses Holmes died on June 4, 1886.

(1884–1889 Registration List)

Fred Buffalo
Ponca
1869–1886

Fred Buffalo, a full Ponca, was 16-years-old when he arrived on August 30, 1884, from Ponca, Indian Territory. Once known as *Ki-la-ge-de*, he was under the guardianship of his uncle Stands Yellow, also from Ponca, Indian Territory. Fred died on June 6, 1886 from consumption.

(1884–1889 Registration List)

Ollie Walker
Cheyenne
1875–1886

Ollie Walker, a 9-year-old female Cheyenne from Darlington, Indian Territory, arrived at Haskell on September 19, 1884; her parent/guardian was Spotted Wolf. Ollie died on December 30, 1886.

(1884–1889 Registration List)

Susie Walker
Cheyenne
1878–1886

Susie Walker, or *His-to-be-yoe*, also arrived on September 19, 1884 from Darlington, Indian Territory; she was 6-years old and her parent/guardian was Mr. Walker. Susie died of consumption on August 29, 1886.

(1884–1889 Registration List)

Sophie Cadue
Kickapoo
1874–1886

Once known as *Mishalgoco*, **Sophia Cadue** was an 11-year-old Kickapoo who arrived on March 14, 1885; her parent/guardian was *Chaptise* from Kickapoo Agency, Kansas. She died on August 19, 1886 from consumption.

(1884–1889 Registration List)

Somebody's Nephew
Unknown
Unknown

Somebody's Niece
Unknown
Unknown

George Clark
Pawnee
1875–1889

A 13-year-old Pawnee, **George Clark** arrived from Pawnee, Indian Territory on April 17, 1888. He died of consumption on May 26, 1889.

(1884–1889 Registration List)

Joseph Banks
Piute
1869–1889

Joseph Banks was a full Paiute from Nevada who arrived on January 7, 1889, at the age of 20. He died on July 20, 1889.

(1884–1889 Registration List)

Webb Hayes
Pawnee
1864–1889

Webb Hayes, or *Tah-wah-tsa-lei-heh-leh*, was a full Pawnee who arrived on December 15, 1886, at the age of 22; his parent/guardian was Sun Chief of Pawnee Agency. Webb died on July 27, 1889 of consumption and pneumonia.

(1884–1889 Registration List)

Lee Hall
Wichita
1874–1899

Lee Hall, a full Wichita from the Kiowa, Comanche and Wichita Agency, arrived at Haskell on February 22, 1889 at the age 15. He was once known as *Gits-a-is*; his parent/guardian was *As-kah-wis*. Lee died of Typho Malaria Fever on October 19, 1889.

(1884–1889 Registration List)

Henry LeClair
Ponca
1874–1890

A full Ponca, **Henry LaClair** was 15 years old when he arrived on October 12, 1888. His parent/guardian was David LaClair from Ponca Agency.

(1884–1889 Registration List)

Ora Mathews
Osage
1875–1890

Annie Dickson
Arapahoe
1871–1890

Jerry Wolfchief
Cheyenne
1875–1891

Jerry Wolfchief, a 13-year-old Cheyenne from Darlington, Indian Territory, arrived at Haskell on March 9, 1888. His parent/guardian was *Red Bird*.

(1884–1889 Registration List)

Christopher Big Joe
Ottawa
1873–1891

Harry Hanneno
Commanche
1868–1891

Harry Hanneno, or *Chah-ah-see*, an 18-year-old full Comanche from Anadarko, Indian Territory, arrived on September 19, 1884; his parent/guardian was *Mah-ah-wa*. After completing a four-year term, Harry "Entered for second term of two years. July 3, 1888."

(1884–1889 Registration List)

Agnes Ricketts
Pawnee
1881–1891

Agnes Ricketts, a full Pawnee, arrived on September 13, 1888 at the age of 6. Her parent/guardian was Clark Rickets from Pawnee Agency.

(1884–1889 Registration List)

Jonah Moharty
Shawnee
1871–1891

Fred Ingalls
Modoc
1878–1892

George Pishabay
Ottawa
1879–1892

Ambrose Pequonca
Ottawa
1874–1895

John Momdoka
Potawatomi
1880–1895

Johnnie Momdoka was a 10-year-old Pottawatomie who arrived on September 25, 1889. His parent/guardian is listed as "Joseph Mamdoka (F), J F Culp (G)" from Athens, Michigan. [F signifies father and G signifies guardian.]

(1884–1889 Registration List)

Nettie Pequah
Kickapoo
1888–1895

Nelson Swamp
Oneida
1887–1899

The following obituary was printed in the May 15, 1899 issue of *The Indian Leader:*

Nelson Swamp

Although not unexpected the death of little **Nelson Swamp** on the morning of May 6 was a shock to many. Nelson was not a strong child as he has suffered for years with some nervous trouble. When the pupils were having the measles a few weeks ago Nelson contracted the disease. Pneumonia followed and in his weak condition he could not rally from it. At times he seemed better, but in spite of medical skill and the best of nursing he grew worse. The end was peaceful. He slept quietly; his breathing became gradually fainted until it ceased. When he awoke it was in another world.

The funeral service was held late in the afternoon and was conducted by Rev. J. W. Somerville, pastor of the Lawrence Methodist church. The coffin was almost covered with beautiful roses by his teacher, Miss Richards; at one end was a wreath of carnations presented by the normal class. Nelson was so fond of flowers that it seemed fitting that there should be many of them around him in his last sleep.   (p. 2)

Josephine Choate
Asiniboin
1878–1899

The following obituary was printed in the October 13, 1899 issue of *The Indian Leader:*

Josephine Choate

Josephine Choate, who was ill at the hospital for more than a year, died in the early morning of October 5. Josephine was an Assiniboine from Wolf Point, Montana. She was very intelligent, extremely fond of reading; remembered what she read and liked to talk about it. During her long illness she was cheerful and patient, having a smile for all who visited her and always grateful to those who cared for her, or brought books, flowers, and other little offerings.

Josephine was a Christian and was ready and anxious to go to the "mansions" in her Father's house. A few days before her death Dr. Dixon asked her to give him a text for the Sunday afternoon service. She said "Tell the boys and girls that it is hard to be always good, but it pays in the end." She also sent her thanks to the girls and others who had been so kind to her.

The funeral services were held at four o'clock in the afternoon, and were conducted by Rev. W. G. Banker, of Lawrence. The casket was covered with exquisite roses brought by employes and Josephine's classmates.   (p. 2)

ROW FOUR, SOUTH END

Cecelia Mae
Fiddler
Chippewa
1923–1943

The following obituary was printed in the February 26, 1943 issue of *The Indian Leader:*

Services for Cecelia Fiddler

Cecelia Fiddler, a Haskell high school student, passed away at the Haskell hospital on February 17, after a long illness. Services were held both at the St. John's Catholic Church in Lawrence and on the Haskell campus.

Cecelia's mother, Mrs. Florence Meunier of Rolla, North Dakota, arrived at Haskell in time to spend the last few weeks with her daughter. Haskell students and employees extend deepest sympathy to Cecelia's family. (p. 3)

ROW FOUR, NORTH END

Infant
son of
Horace & Emma
Randel
Nov 29, 1904

There is no mention of the death of an infant in the first December 1904 issue of Haskell's campus newspaper. However, there is mention of sickness in the Randel household in the month of November. Then the following obituary was printed in the December 16, 1904 issue of *The Indian Leader:*

At Rest

Mrs. Horace Randel, who has been ill for the past three weeks with measles, followed by pneumonia, entered into rest Tuesday morning a little after two o'clock. From the first her illness was serious and the devoted care of her husband, parents, skilled physician, trained nurse and friends was of no avail.

Mrs. Randel came here with her husband when he was appointed assistant carpenter a little more than a year ago, and by her gentle ways and sweet retiring disposition had endeared herself to all who came to know her.

The young husband, father and mother and other relatives have the heartfelt sympathy of the employees and pupils in their great sorrow.

(p. 4)

ROW FIVE, NORTH TO SOUTH

Antonio Prieto
Mission
1895–1911

The following obituary was printed in the November 17, 1911 issue of *The Indian Leader:*

Antonio Prieto

Antonio Prieto, a pupil from California, died on November 7, of peritonitis, aged fourteen. He was a pleasant, obedient boy, much liked by his teachers and associates. Last year he was a faithful member of the Volunteers attending regularly on Sunday evenings. Antonio was an orphan. An older brother, Otheno, is a pupil here. The funeral service occurred in chapel Thursday afternoon, conducted by Rev. G. J. Eckart.

At the close of the service the pupils were lined up on either side of the walk in front of the chapel and stood silently with uncovered heads, while the white casket, covered with beautiful yellow and white chrysanthemums, was carried to the conveyance that bore it to the school cemetery, followed by the little company of which he was a member.   (p. 2)

Thomas Little Wolf
Sioux
1897–1908

Sadie Miles
Miami
1893–1907

The following obituary was printed in the April 19, 1907 issue of *The Indian Leader:*

Sadie Miles, aged fourteen, was "called away" last Friday morning. She was a great favorite with her companions, many of whom were overcome with grief when they learned of her death. The officer in charge of her company said she never had to report Sadie, as she was always courteous, pleasant and well-behaved. Mr. Miles came Friday morning, but too late. Rev. Father Eckhardt conducted the funeral service. There were many beautiful flowers, the offering of different friends. The parents, brothers and sister, have the sincere sympathy of friends at Haskell.   (p. 3)

Leland
Son of
Dennis & Louise
Wheelock
Born Jan. 28 1902
Died Jan. 25 1903

Dennis Wheelock was a full-blood Oneida who arrived at Haskell in 1902 as an assistant disciplinarian. Formerly a band leader at Carlisle, he led the Haskell band to new heights.

Ablicio Sena
Navaho
1890–1907

The following obituary was printed in the March 8, 1907 issue of *The Indian Leader:*

The death angel entered out midst last Friday and carried home one of our dearest little boys, **Ablyssio Sena**. "To know him was to love him" and little Ablyssio's friends were many. He was quiet, pleasant, industrious and painstaking. One of his ambitions was to learn to speak English well. The funeral was held on Sunday afternoon. Father Eckhardt and a visiting priest were in charge. The members of company I, to which Ablyssio belonged, several employes and officers were in attendance and accompanied the remains of their little friend to the cemetery. The floral offerings by the little one's teacher, matron and other friends were beautiful. The parents at their home in New Mexico have the sympathy of Haskell friends in their great sorrow.

(p. 3)

Patrick Levali
Chippewa
1889–1907

The following obituary was printed in the January 25, 1907 issue of *The Indian Leader:*

The death of **Patrick Levale** from peritonitis on the morning of January 17, was a shock to all. Patrick came to Haskell last October from North Dakota, where he had attended the Fort Totten school. He was seventeen years of age and was in Sixth grade. He was quiet, nice boy and well liked by his companions. The sympathy of Patrick's friends here is extended to his family in their sorrow.   (p. 3)

David Hanson
Digger
1890–1910

John Little Eyes
N. Cheyenne
1881–1905

The following obituary was printed in the March 24, 1905 issue of *The Indian Leader:*

John Little Eyes, a Cheyenne boy from Montana, fell a victim to the dread disease, quick consumption, last Friday evening. He had been out of school but four weeks and it is hard to realize that he has gone from us. John did not speak English fluently and seldom talked unless questioned, but he was fond of studying and of drawing. He was a boy who never gave trouble and spent a great deal of his spare time in the reading room, reading or looking at the pictures in the magazines. The funeral service Saturday afternoon was conducted by Rev. Stauffler of Lawrence.   (p. 2)

Sophia Webster
Oneida
1890–1905

The following obituary was printed in the January 6, 1905 issue of *The Indian Leader:*

Sophie Webster
The first day of the New Year was saddened by the loss of one of our dear pupils—bright-eyed, pleasant-faced, cheery Sophie Webster. Her death came as a shock for she had been ill but a short time.

Sophie had been a pupil here for a year and a half and was loved by her teachers and companions. Her great wish was to be helpful, and during her illness she talked of helping her father after she finished the course in school. She was only fifteen, so young to go away it seemed to her friends. But the dear Father in Heaven was wiser than they and took her to be with Him, where the sorrows that troubled her here will never be thought of again and where all is joy.

Rev. Baxter, her pastor in the Episcopal church, conducted the beautiful funeral service Monday afternoon.

Friends of the same tribe—Oneida—acted as pall-bearers, and followed by her classmates the mortal part of Sophie was laid to rest in the little cemetery.   (p. 2)

Somebody
Unknown
Unknown

Gorman Carter
Caddo
1886–1904

Chas. Roughfeather
Sioux
1886–1904

The following obituary was printed in the June 10, 1904 issue of *The Indian Leader:*

Charles Roughfeather
Charles Roughfeather, aged eighteen, died of rheumatism of the heart on May 29, mourned by teachers and schoolmates. He was an industrious, thoughtful boy and anxious to learn. Hours of his time were spent in the reading room reading and studying in connection with his school work.

A few hours before his death he said to his teacher that he wished to get well, but if he could not he was ready to go; ready to trust all to the Savior.

Charles' teacher said of him: "He always did his best in everything he was asked to do." Could anyone do more?

Charles was a Pine Ridge Sioux and was a favorite with both white people and Indians on the reservation. (p. 2)

Barrett Longmarsh
Winnebago
1886–1904

The following obituary was printed in the May 27, 1904 issue of *The Indian Leader:*

Barrett Longmarsh a Winnebago boy aged about seventeen, died Saturday morning of kidney trouble. He was ill but three days and then not confined to his bed much of the time. This is the first death that has occurred at Haskell for a year and a half and coming with so little warning was a great shock to Barrett's many friends. (p. 3)

Luella Bronson
Delaware
1892–1902

Willie Hanson
Winnebago
1882–1902

Joseph Rousseau
Chippewa
1886–1902

The following obituary was printed in the October 17, 1902 issue of *The Indian Leader:*

Joseph Rosseau
With the falling of the Autumn leaves another of our dear pupils, **Joseph Rosseau,** "at the age twixt boy and youth," has been called, after but a few days of illness, from his busy life here to another world. Joseph was one of the reliable boys. He worked in the boiler house, was always industrious and seemed to thoroughly enjoy being busy. When any duty was assigned him there was no shirking. Superinten-

dent Peairs said: "If we told Joseph to do anything we knew it would be done; we could always depend upon him." In school it was the same. The teachers who have had him in their classes in the years he has been here have only words of praise for him; he was studious, obedient, pleasant, intelligent — a model pupil. His devotion to his little sisters and his younger brother was often commented on. One of his teachers said: "I have seen many good brothers, but never one quite as kind as Joseph. He seemed to be so thoughtful for the other children; so anxious to give them pleasure."

Joseph seemed to realize that death was near saying to the nurse: "I'll not be here much longer."

Rev. Downey, pastor of the Catholic church in Lawrence, conducted the impressive funeral service. There were beautiful floral offerings from Joseph's teacher, his classmates and his brother Paul.

(p. 2)

Lomo Congwio
Hopi
1884–1902

There apparently is no obituary for Lomo. However, there are two entries in *The Indian Leader* that tell a little story about the young man:

Lomo Congwhio, of Keam's Canon, Arizona, entered school the first of the week. He wished some months ago to come to Haskell, but was told that transportation could not be furnished. This did not discourage him in the least. He went to work, saved his money, and paid his own way, the expenses being between forty and fifty dollars. Certainly he has the pluck and perseverance that will make him successful in getting an education in books and in the industrial departments.

(*IL*, February 1, 1901, p. 3)

Lomo Congwhio is now working in the pupils' kitchen.

(*IL*, May 24, 1901, p. 3)

Charles Quein
Wyandotte
1883–1902

John Taylor
Ute
1876–1902

The following obituary was printed in the February 28, 1902 issue of *The Indian Leader:*

John Taylor, who had been ill for some time, died of consumption last Tuesday night and was buried Wednesday afternoon. He was a quiet boy and well liked by those who came to know and understand him. He was fond of writing stories and showed considerable talent in this line. He was a member of the Y.M.C.A. and said a short time before his death that he was a Christian and was willing to trust his future to the Lord. Dr. Dixon conducted the solemn funeral service. The floral offerings from his teacher and other friends were beautiful. His sister Laura, who was with him a great deal during his illness, has the sincere sympathy of her friends.   (p. 3)

Willie Burnett
Potawatomi
1886–1901

Andrew Smith
E. Cherokee
1876–1901

The following obituary was printed in the December 20, 1901 issue of *The Indian Leader:*

Andrew Smith

Another dear friend has fallen asleep and many hearts are saddened. After a long illness Andrew Smith, a Northern Cherokee aged about twenty, passed away last Sunday evening. Andrew was a boy who had many friends. He was quiet, gentlemanly, cheerful and industrious. He had worked in the tailor shop for two years and his instructor said in that time he never once had occasion to reprove him or to criticise him. He was always the same happy, willing, neat, steady worker.

Andrew's former teacher thought him one of the best boys she had ever known—a beautiful character. His teacher this year said of him, "Andrew is such a good boy; if he has any spare minutes he takes out his little Testament and reads."

At his home in North Carolina Andrew was a member of the Baptist church and his last request was that Rev. Russell, the pastor of the Baptist church in Lawrence, should conduct the funeral service. This request was granted. Mr. Russell read the ninetieth psalm and his sermon upon life, death and eternity was solemn and impressive. Dr. Dixon added a few remarks in regard to Andrew's upright Christian character and said that his last words were a prayer.

Beautiful flowers from his teachers in school and industrial department and his classmates were laid in profusion upon the coffin.

In the little cemetery Andrew's body was laid to rest on Monday afternoon, but his spirit had entered the golden chamber of the King whom he served here.   (p. 3)

Job Long
E. Cherokee
1883–1901

The following obituary was printed in the November 29, 1901 issue of *The Indian Leader:*

At Rest

Job Long, a Cherokee boy of seventeen, from North Carolina, died on Saturday morning of pneumonia. Job was a quiet, good, industrious boy, a comfort to his teacher and well-liked by his companions. His last words were that he was ready to go. He was a Baptist and the funeral service was conducted by Mr. Russell, pastor of the Baptist church in Lawrence. Beautiful white chrysanthemums were the floral tributes. The music by the choir was appropriate and the sermon was full of beautiful, helpful, comforting thoughts.   (p. 2)

Caleb Lew
Ukie
1895–1913

NO TOMBSTONES—Where Did They Go?

The first three individuals are listed in the 1884–1889 Haskell student registration ledger. The information on each is presented.

Edward Harrold

Edward Harold, or *Wah-wah*, was a full Arapahoe who arrived on December 4, 1884 at the age of 19; his parent/guardian was Left Hand from Darlington, Indian Territory. Edward died on February 11, 1885 of consumption.

(1884–1889 Registration List)

John Curley

John Curley, once known as *Con-gee*, was a ¾ Pottawatomie who arrived on October 28, 1884 when he was 17-years-old; *We-Zo* from Osage Agency, Indian Territory was his parent/guardian. John died of typho-malaria on August 23, 1886.

(1884–1889 Registration List)

Jennie Lizzard

Jennie Lizzard, or *Mahenoch*, was 17-years-old when she arrived in September 1884. A full Arapahoe, her parent/guardian was Lizzard from Darlington, Indian Territory. Jennie died of consumption on March 11, 1887.

(1884–1889 Registration List)

The following obituary was printed in the February 10, 1911 issue of *The Indian Leader:*

Roman Harjo

Roman Harjo, a Creek boy, aged eighteen, died last Saturday morning after an illness of only a few days. His home was at Sasakwa, Oklahoma. Although he had been in school but little and was a second grade pupil he was anxious to learn and was always quiet, obedient and studious. He would write his lessons over and over again in order to have them neat.

The funeral service was held in chapel Sunday afternoon. The choir sang appropriate selections and Dr. Wolfe's short sermon was most earnest and impressive.

The casket was covered with beautiful flowers from a number of the boys. The burial was in the school cemetery.   (p. 2)

Theresa Milk, Lakota wife, mother and grandmother, received her Associate of Arts and Bachelor of Arts degrees from Haskell Indian Nations University. While at Haskell, she was active with *the Indian Leader*. In 2000, she was selected as an inaugural Gates Scholar, which allowed her to continue her education. She then attended the University of Kansas School of Education for her Masters degree and Ph.D. She received the Crystal Eagle Award from the KU Indigenous Nations Studies Program in 2007. She has taught English and American Indian Studies courses at Haskell since 2001.